The book *Four Blood Moons: Your Future Begins Now!* by Pastor Larry Huch is a spiritual and prophetic on time book for the church today. It's a relevant word for unlocking the keys to the four blood moons occurrences. The corresponding Scriptures show how these supernatural events tie directly into the biblical principles of the favor and blessings of God in these last days. Pastor Larry provides the reader with insights into these significant "events in the sky" never addressed before. It is a treasure chest revealing the heart of God, and His plans for the Church in the end time.

—Marcus D. Lamb
Founder-President
Daystar Television Network

4 BLOOD
MOONS

LARRY HUCH

4 BLOOD MOONS

YOUR **FUTURE** BEGINS **NOW!**

POWER
PROPHECY
AND
PROSPERITY

WINTERS
PUBLISHING GROUP

Published by Winters Publishing, LLC
2448 E. 81st St. Suite #4802 | Tulsa, Oklahoma 74137 USA

Book design copyright © 2014 by Winters Publishing, LLC. All rights reserved.
Cover design by Eileen Cueno
Interior design by Jimmy Sevilleno

Published in the United States of America

ISBN: 978-1-63367-103-4
1. Religion/Christianity/General
2. Religion/Judaism/General
14.09.11

I dedicate this book to my children and their spouses, who have always shared our passion for God, His Word, His people, and our ministry. I'm so proud of each one of you—as a wonderful person and as an integral part of our ministry team. Anna and Brandin (spouse), Luke and Jen (spouse), and Katie....you validate my purpose, and you fill my life with love and fun!

To my "grandsugars," Asher, Judah, and Aviva Shalom, the light and joy of my life.

And, as always, to my wife, Tiz, who, for more than thirty-seven years, has brought continual inspiration, support, and love to everything I do.

CONTENTS

Introduction 11

1 When Science Proves the Bible 15

2 How History Impacts Our World Today 33

3 A Phenomenal Prophet and His Incredible Prophecy! 47

4 The Miracle of Shemittah and Jubilee 59

5 The Wake-Up Call: Sounding the Alarm! 77

6 Prosperity, Tzedakah, and Repairing a Broken World 85

7 The Blessing of the Old Paths and Appointed Times 101

8 The Blood Moons and the Power of Pentecost 113

9 End-Time Prophecies for the Church and Israel 133

10 The Dawn of the Messianic Era 155

About the Author 165

Books by Pastor Larry Huch 167

INTRODUCTION

In the ancient Hebrew language, there is no word for coincidence. This means if you're reading this book today, it's not by accident. God has purposely caused things to happen for you to connect with the greatest end-time biblical revelation. It's God's revelation that will inform you, prepare you, and bless you with a great outpouring of wisdom, wealth, and influence like you've never seen before and will never see again.

The reason the Lord spoke to me to write this book is found in Isaiah 19:20: "And it will be for a sign and for a witness to the LORD of hosts in the land of Egypt; for they will cry to the LORD because of the oppressors, and He will send them a Savior and a Mighty One, and He will deliver them."

I knew in my heart He would help teach you things He has saved for the end times. The Lord showed me that what is happening in the skies throughout 2014 and 2015 would launch His people into the greatest of times. I saw how these four "blood moons"—lunar eclipses named for the color the moon appears as it darkens—and how they occur on specific biblical holidays contain secrets that will usher in great opportunity in your life and phenomenal change in the world. We have had blood moons before but never like this—like now.

One of the fascinating truths you will discover is right now, in what seems to be a first, science is validating the Word of God. In other words, God has chosen this time in history to reveal certain prophetic signs to serve as proof His Word is true. Now, through a fresh understanding of biblical prophecy, you will be connected to a whole new dimension of God's power, promises, and prosperity—things you will need to thrive in these last days. In His great mercy and grace, God is shouting to wake up and pay attention because the world—your world—is about to change.

What makes these four blood moons so unique and important is that since the time that Jesus died on the cross and was resurrected until right now, there have been seven occurrences of four consecutive blood moons falling on biblical holidays; specifically on the Bible Feasts of Passover and Feast of Tabernacles (Sukkot). Let me say this again, this has only happened seven times since Jesus.

Biblically, the number seven means completion. It signifies God's completed purpose with man. Right now we've entered into the eighth series of blood moons which represents a new beginning. Eight symbolizes man's ability to transcend all physical boundaries and limitations. As one leading rabbi recently said, we are now living in a ripe moment.

NASA and the scientific community have reported this phenomenon of the blood moons. However, they don't realize the spiritual significance of it all. The earth, the sun, and the moon must be in a rare and specific alignment that has seldom happened in human history. It goes beyond all mathematical possibilities. What we all need to realize is God has caused these blood moon dates to materialize as a sign to His creation things are about to change!

One of the reasons the Lord had me write this book is that too many times books on prophecy and the end times emphasize the doom and gloom. This tends to cause a certain amount of fear and anxiety in people. However, God does not want us to live in fear, He wants us to live in faith and positive expectation. As I'm going to show you, this is not going to be the worst of times for God's people, but the best of times, because our redemption is drawing near.

I love to tell people that when you read God's Word you need to put on Jewish glasses. The Bible is best understood when you realize that it was given by a Jewish God, written by Jewish men, and that we receive eternal life through a Jewish Messiah. As we go through this book together, my prayer is that God gives you Jewish eyes—Hebrew eyes—so you can receive the fullest meaning of the scriptures. You will learn how God is revealing ancient biblical secrets—mysteries to the church world for centuries—at this time in history so you can receive the promises and prophecies of the Bible at the highest levels.

Believe me, this is my greatest hope and desire for you. As these signs in heaven continue to appear, as you grow in your knowledge of God's end-time plan, I sincerely believe you will experience an acceleration in wisdom, faith, and spiritual vision that will guide you through any challenge or difficulty and into an outpouring of God's blessing, power, and miracles. Your world, as you are reading, is about to change. Your future has already begun!

1

When Science Proves the Bible

And I will show wonders in the heavens and in the earth:
blood and fire and pillars of smoke. The sun shall be
turned into darkness, and the moon into blood, before
the coming of the great and awesome day of the Lord.

—Joel 2:30–31

The fact that you picked up this book tells me one thing about you: you want to go deeper into the study of the Word of God. Obviously the news of the blood moons captured your attention and the Holy Spirit has prompted you to search for the godly knowledge, wisdom, and discernment you need to flourish in these end times.

You see, this season of blood moons, these signs in heaven are a strong and clear signal from God. But what does all of this mean for you and your future? While much has been written on this subject, I can guarantee you this book is unlike anything you've ever read. For one, I don't think all these things are aligning to predict something negative or chaotic. Rather, I believe God can and will use this to bring about something very positive, something that's going to change your life for the better and change the world we live in forever.

Yet, if these are going to be the best of times, it's vital that we have eyes to see the four blood moons are a sign from God! The first blood moon was on Passover 2014, the second blood moon is on Sukkot, the Feast of Tabernacles 2014, the third blood moon is on Passover 2015, and then comes Jubilee and the fourth blood moon on the Feast of Tabernacles 2015. This is not a coincidence!

Jesus told His disciples, "But blessed are your eyes for they see, and your ears for they hear; for assuredly, I say to you that many prophets and righteous men desired to see what you see, and did not see it, and to hear what you hear, and did not hear it" (Matthew 13:16–17).

Of course, the Lord is talking about having spiritual eyes and spiritual vision. Unfortunately, the world, including much of the Christian world, isn't living like the Lord could return any day. People are going to miss these blood moons and the many other things the Lord is doing as that great day approaches. They have eyes but they won't see it. They have ears but they won't hear it. My prayer is that you, your family, your church, and the body of the Christ around the world will see what God is doing and respond.

REDEMPTION IS CLOSER THAN YOU THINK

So what exactly are we to do when we see these signs in the heavens? Jesus gave some very clear instructions: "Now when these things begin to happen, look up and lift up your heads, because your redemption draws near" (Luke 21:28).

Look up and lift up your heads! Why? *Because your redemption is at hand!* For those of us who see God's end-time plan, it will first and foremost lead us into redemption. When we think of redemption in religious terms, we typically think it means eternity, heaven, and life in the world to come. While that is true, there is so much more meaning in this verse that I want you to see, and in order for you to see it, I need to teach you some things from a Hebrew mindset. Again this is one key reason why this book is so distinctive: you're going to learn biblical truths most of the Church has never been taught because we have been separated from our Hebraic or Jewish roots of Christianity.

Let's look at Luke 21:28 again: "Look up and lift up your heads." At first glance, it appears to be repetitive—if you *look up,* don't you automatically have to *lift up your heads?* So why did Jesus repeat himself? It's because in ancient Hebrew tradition, when something is repeated back-to-back in Scripture—just like this—it means there is a secret to be revealed.

When Jesus says, "Look up," He is talking about physically looking up—fixing your eyes on the heavens, looking for signs in the skies. In His great love and compassion for us, the Lord doesn't want us to miss out on what is about to happen. What Jesus is saying is that as these various signs of the end times begin to happen, get ready because something powerful is about to occur.

But then Jesus repeats Himself by saying, "Lift up your heads." It's here He reveals the secret in this, not a physical response but a spiritual response to these signs—when you see these things begin to happen, don't be discouraged or downcast. Lift up your heads in faith and with confidence because you have a living hope and strong expectation of our coming redemption.

Notice too that it's as these signs *begin* to happen that we need to anticipate redemption. So often Christians have the mistaken idea that redemption is a last-second rescue operation, that we need to hide out and hang on until the Lord returns. But redemption is more than just entering into eternity. While it's true that eternity is the ultimate goal, our redemption is meant to start with you and me living an abundant life now.

Jesus said, "The thief does not come except to steal, and to kill, and to destroy. I have come that they may have life, and that they may have it more abundantly" (John 10:10).

Redemption and "being redeemed" not only means salvation and deliverance in eternity, it also means to be brought back to our original state in this world. The true biblical definition of redemption includes God bringing us back to the state of mankind before Adam sinned. In this state, sin, sickness, and poverty have no place. Only God's power, promises, and provision in overflowing abundance are meant to surround us and cover us. This is part of God's end-time plan. It includes restoring us to that place of blessing and favor that we in the Church have known as the latter rain (which we'll discuss later).

So, there is no doubt our redemption and the miracles and breakthroughs like we've never seen before are drawing near. I can confidently say that as we close in on eternity, the Church will not go into a period of weakness, sickness, and failure, but one of incredible blessing and prosperity, specifically for those who have eyes to see and ears to hear.

Ephesians 5:27 says, "That He might present her to Himself a glorious church, not having spot or wrinkle or any such thing, but that she should be holy and without blemish."

At the end of days when Jesus comes again, He's coming for a glorious Church. This term, "glorious church," tells us what condition the Church will be in when this world as we know it comes to an end and the Lord returns. A glorious Church speaks of God manifesting the fullness of everything the Bible promises.

For those who receive this revelation, it puts them on a pathway of living in divine health, living under divine prosperity, and experiencing signs, wonders, and miracles so that the whole world will see and say, "Truly He is the Son of the living God!" I believe we're entering into that season right now and He's going to bring about amazing things as our redemption is at hand.

BIBLICAL EXAMPLES OF SIGNS IN THE HEAVENS

When God tells us in His Word to look for the signs in the heavens, He is talking about astronomy, not astrology. Astronomy is a real science based on observation and research that studies the stars, the moon, and the planets—everything outside the earth's atmosphere. It's considered one of the oldest sciences and many of the oldest civilizations in world history have studied the skies. In fact, our very own Bible is filled with examples of this very thing.

Then God said, "Let there be lights in the firmament
of the heavens to divide the day from the night; and let
them be for signs and seasons, and for days and years."
(Genesis 1:14)

We are told about signs in the heavens from the time of
creation. The biblical definition of the word *signs* in Genesis 1
means "a signal, a flag, a beacon, an omen, evidence, a miracle,
sign or token." God is saying let the lights in the sky be a signal and evidence for you.

When God called Abraham, the Father of our Faith,
He used the stars to illustrate that there would be no lim-
its to Abraham's heritage and legacy: "Then He brought him
[Abraham] outside and said, 'Look now toward heaven, and
count the stars if you are able to number them'" (Genesis 15:5).

Again, in speaking to Joseph in a dream, God used the
skies as the way to convey Joseph's spiritual destiny: "Then he
dreamed still another dream and told it to his brothers, and
said, 'Look, I have dreamed another dream. And this time,
the sun, the moon, and the eleven stars bowed down to me'"
(Genesis 37:9).

Let's not forget one of the most extraordinary events in
all of human history—the birth of Jesus. In the well-known
biblical account in Matthew 2, we see that God used a star to

lead the wise men from the east. Verse 2 says, "Where is He who has been born King of the Jews? For we have seen His star in the East and have come to worship Him."

These wise men had a keen knowledge of biblical prophecy and understood the star was a sign in the heavens signaling the birth of a King. They responded in faith to what God was showing them, took corresponding action, and followed the star all the way to Bethlehem, where they found the child laying in a manger.

In Matthew 2:11, this teaching goes on to say, "And when they had come into the house, they saw the young Child with Mary His mother, and fell down and worshiped Him. When they had opened their treasures, they presented gifts to Him: gold, frankincense, and myrrh."

During the first coming of Jesus, these wise men knew prophetically the world was about to change and responded. I believe the signs we see today are telling us that we are in the season just before the second coming of Jesus. I'm not predicting when Jesus will return because no man knows the exact day or hour, however, the Bible says for those of us who are looking, we will know the season. I believe we're in that season now and the blood moons serve as powerful evidence of this very thing.

THE SCIENCE OF ASTRONOMY (NOT ASTROLOGY) MEETS THE BIBLE

The discovery of the sequence of these four blood moons is pretty amazing. Even the world's most renowned astronomers—those who work for NASA—are writing about it. Science is confirming the Bible in ways we've never seen before. When the Bible has spoken of the sun darkening, science has explained solar eclipses to us. When the Bible has forecast a blood-colored moon, science has explained lunar eclipses to us. Astronomers have recorded these phenomena going all the way back in history. They're also able to look forward to see scientifically when they will occur again.

Blood moons, or total lunar eclipses, are fairly common. They occur when the moon is fully in the earth's shadow and light from the sun is bent toward the moon through the earth's atmosphere, resulting in a burnt orange or red lighting of the moon. But what is not at all common is what we're talking about in this book—four consecutive blood moons occurring exactly on biblical holidays, or the Feasts of the Lord.

This very rare phenomenon is known as an astronomical tetrad—or four blood moons in series. NASA confirms it has happened only seven times since the time of Jesus Christ. Seven—the biblical number of perfection and completion. What's so profound is NASA has looked forward as far as they can see, and there is not another tetrad aligning on these holy days. This is it!

Not only that, but NASA goes on to forecast this tetrad of blood moons will correspond exactly with the biblical celebrations of Passover and the Feast of Tabernacles (Sukkot) in both 2014 and 2015.

This will be just the eighth time this has happened in two thousand years—and as you may know, eight represents a new beginning. Each time in history these blood moons have occurred, the world greatly changed and something powerful began. So as this eighth series happens, God is saying, "It's not the end of what I'm doing, I'm about to bring you and the world a new beginning!"

Let me set the actual calendar for you again. The first of these four blood moons occurred on Passover, April 15, 2014. The second blood moon is on October 8, 2014, the first day of Sukkot, the Feast of Tabernacles. The third blood moon will occur on April 4, 2015, again on the first day of Passover. The fourth and final blood moon happens on September 28, 2015, again on the first day of Sukkot. NASA has also forecasted that there will be a total solar eclipse between the second and the third blood moons, on March 20, 2015. A solar eclipse happens when the moon passes between the sun and the earth, blocking the sun's light.

According to NASA, these four blood moons will not be seen everywhere, every time. In fact, Israel will only see the last blood moon. But they'll see it during Sukkot, the Feast of Tabernacles. What makes this so powerful is that on Sukkot every Jew throughout Israel (and Jews around the world, for that matter) builds a temporary shelter outside of their house called a *succah*. God commanded Israel to build these annually as part of the festival.

The purpose of the succah is to remind each person that this world is just temporary. Throughout the entire seven-day celebration, each person spends as much time as possible in the shelter. It serves as a way to connect to Israel's time in the wilderness when they had to totally rely and depend on God. Some have called it the "shelter of faith" because God provided everything by His love and grace: manna from heaven, water from a rock, divine guidance, and protection. God provided it all on the journey to the Promised Land.

This is the reason why, when building a succah, the roof is not fully enclosed. It is left somewhat open so you can always have a view of the sky. Your focus and attention is always upward, looking to the heavens, remembering the Lord and constantly looking for a sign from God that the Messiah is coming. The blood moons serve as such a sign. As we see on Joel 2:31: "The sun shall be turned into darkness, and the moon into blood, before the coming of the great and awesome day of the LORD."

The apostle Peter echoed Joel in his message on Pentecost: "I will show wonders in heaven above and signs in the earth beneath: blood and fire and vapor of smoke. The sun shall be turned into darkness, and the moon into blood, before the coming of the great and awesome day of the LORD" (Acts 2:19–20).

When Joel prophesied about the sun darkening and the moon turning to blood, and when Peter quoted Joel, they had no idea about science, eclipses, and NASA, and yet what they spoke of is happening nonetheless. The rarity of the sun, moon, and earth all aligning in solar eclipses and lunar eclipses exactly with the biblical holidays is, at the very least, a mathematical improbability.

Now with this eighth tetrad of four blood moons there are even more reasons: prophecies, the Shemittah and Jubilee lining up exactly as God and His prophets said, making it almost an impossibility, except for one thing, *God said it*!

THE TIME AND SEASON FOR A MIRACLE HARVEST

I've been teaching the Jewish roots of Christianity and the revelation of the biblical holidays since the mid-nineties. Sadly, many Christians haven't been told that God has exact seasons on His calendar when He will open the window of blessing over us like no other time of the year. As I've written in my previous books, *The Torah Blessing* and *Unveiling Ancient Biblical Secrets*, God has set these exact times in place to bless His people. These are called the appointed times or in Hebrew, the *moedim*.

These are special seasons on God's calendar when He does unusual and extraordinary things. As we see in Malachi 3, God tells us He will open the windows of heaven and pour out His blessings. Those windows, which in Hebrew are called *yeshods*, or *yesods*, are to be opened three times a year, on Passover, Pentecost (Shavuot in Hebrew), and Feast of Tabernacles (Sukkot).

Each holiday features its own unique and powerful blessing. God is using this amazing sequence of the blood moons falling on the Feasts of the Lord to give us an incredible sign. He is saying "Look up and lift up your heads" because great and mighty things are about to happen!

From the very start, God established that there would be specific times for sowing and reaping. I already showed you Genesis 1:14 where God refers to the signs and the seasons. In Genesis 8:22, God emphasizes, "While the earth remains, seedtime and harvest, cold and heat, winter and summer, and day and night shall not cease."

In Ecclesiastes 3:1, King Solomon writes, "To everything there is a season, A time for every purpose under heaven." These seasons are much more than just winter, spring, summer and fall. Solomon is speaking of the appointed times—supernatural times when God promises an outpouring of spiritual and financial blessing.

One of the great chapters in the Bible is Leviticus 23. Here God dedicates the entire section to explaining these biblical seasons. They are intended to teach us His plan of redemption. Yet it's important to understand that everything God shows has two parts: the heavenly and the earthly, the spiritual and the physical. So while these Feasts of the Lord definitely reveal God's spiritual plan to send the Messiah, they also show us an earthly, physical, or financial plan. A big part of God's strategy to bless us is centered on these Feasts and the special offerings given during these seasons.

This is one of the reasons why the blood moons fall on the biblical holidays. God is connecting these signs in the heavens with the celebrations of Passover and Sukkot because it's an ordained time for both sowing and reaping. Read Deuteronomy 16:1–17 to learn more on this, but in verse 16, God says three times a year on Passover, Pentecost (Shavuot) and Sukkot "you come before Me and don't come before Me empty-handed." Each of these are known as First Fruit offerings and will release an outpouring of blessing as described in Malachi 3.

We'll get into this much more later, but what I want you to see right now is the biblical connection between the blood moons, the Feasts of the Lord, and how your world will change spiritually and financially. God has these events coming into perfect alignment so the miracles associated with these appointed times are magnified—the effects will be multiplied! It will be a great end-time transfer of wealth like we've never seen before.

Let me reiterate one more time—there have been seven blood moons (tetrads) on the biblical holidays since the time of Christ. Seven equals completion. This one is number eight. Eight is a new beginning! The number eight represents a time when man lives above what is natural. It's the beginning of a supernatural season, the greatest time in history, and it won't stop for those of us who have eyes to see until the Messiah returns.

MORE BIBLICAL SIGNS ARE CONVERGING

Since day four of creation, when God set the sun and the moon in place and identified them as signs, He has utilized them to signal something great. But as we're going to discover, there are more signs than just what we're seeing in the heavens. At the same time these four blood moons occur, there is also a coming together of some additional biblical events that elevate this entire sequence to a much higher level.

As we're all learning, there are secrets in the Bible we've missed but God is showing us incredible things to prepare us for an outpouring of blessing. In addition to the signs of the blood moons, there is something else that's going to happen that has never happened before on God's calendar. It's in association with the biblical holiday of Rosh Hashanah, which is also known as the Feast of Trumpets. Rosh Hashanah means "the head of the year" and is considered a biblical New Year. In 2014, Rosh Hashanah is on September 24, and coincides with what is known in the Bible as the beginning of a "Shemittah" year.

The Shemittah year is the seventh year in a seven-year cycle when God says let the land lay fallow, do no planting. It's considered a Sabbath year, a year of rest for the land of Israel. In a physical and agricultural sense, this is so the land has a chance to renew itself for the coming years of harvest.

But at the same time, there is also a key spiritual application: God gives us Shemittah so that we will always remember that we need to trust in Him as Jehovah Jireh, our Provider. It's a clear reminder we need to live by faith.

Now what makes this specific season of time even more amazing is that the very next year, on September 23, 2015, on Yom Kippur, the Day of Atonement, we enter into what the Bible calls a Jubilee year. Again we'll discuss this in detail later but Jubilee on God's calendar is a time of supernatural debt cancellation and total restoration. It's when everything that has been stolen is returned and everything that has been lost is restored.

What this all means to you and I is that there is a strong connection between these four blood moons, Shemittah, and Jubilee. God is using these events to shout to the world things are about to change. For those of us who are looking and listening, it is signaling the coming of a great outpouring of blessing, a great transfer of wealth, and what the prophet Joel called the former and the latter rain. Do you see how all this is lining up?

So, we've entered the season of the eighth series of four blood moons. They correspond exactly with two of the greatest of all the biblical holidays, Passover and Sukkot. Now we've discovered it is linked together with two other powerful but little known biblical events known as Shemittah and Jubilee—you just can't make this up.

What are the odds of four blood moons coming right at this time? What are the odds that we're going into the eighth series of blood moons? What are the odds that these four blood moons would fall exactly on the biblical holidays of Passover and Sukkot? What are the mathematical probabilities these would correspond with the Shemittah and Jubilee years? But in fact, it's what our God has set in place on His divine calendar, and even scientists see it and confirm it. These are amazing times! May we all "look up" and have eyes to see—our redemption draws near!

2

How History Impacts Our World Today

But blessed are your eyes for they see, and your ears for they hear; for assuredly, I say to you that many prophets and righteous men desired to see what you see, and did not see it, and to hear what you hear, and did not hear it.

—Matthew 13:16–17

Throughout my years in ministry, it has always taken a lot to get me to speak on prophecy. I've studied it and taught it, but I haven't been one to get all caught up in it. It is important to be sure, but not that essential for addressing the practical, real-life issues my congregation faces every day. I've always been more focused on what God is doing right now than with what He's going to do in the future.

But in recent months, as I came to understand the significance of the four blood moons and how they line up with history and prophecy, I have become convinced—more convinced than ever—that God is using these signs to show us something, to say something to us. This season of blood moons is what God is doing right now so we need to pay attention, or as Jesus said, "Have eyes to see."

I recently had a dream that illustrates what we're teaching on, and I need to share it with you now. Those who know me well will tell you that, in all these years, I've shared a dream or a vision just a handful of times. Yet this dream was so impactful I need to share it. In fact, when I woke up, I wasn't sure it was a dream at all—it seemed so real.

In my dream, the swimming pool in my backyard was only half full. It was so vivid that I woke up with the image of the pool still lingering in my mind. For some reason, I knew I had to make sure everything was okay, that half my pool water hadn't drained out. So I immediately got up out of bed, put on my robe and slippers, and walked out into the cold winter night to look at the pool.

Even in the dim light I could see the water level was just fine—the pool was full. But as I started to turn around and head back inside the house, something caught my eye: the pipes around the pool equipment were three-quarters frozen. I couldn't shake the feeling something was wrong. I went around the corner of my house to look at the pool's plumbing and found a valve hadn't shut off and indeed the pipes were three-quarters frozen.

Had I not had that dream, those pipes would have frozen and broken the plumbing. In the dream I saw the damage that was about to happen but I had to get up and see, then God showed me what to do and it all turned out great. This actually happened while I was teaching my church here in Dallas on the coming four blood moons. The Lord kept saying to my spirit—those who have eyes to see.

That experience spoke to my heart. I thought, *This is what God is doing*. The prophecies in the Bible, the things that are going on in the world around us, the four blood moons and the significance of their timing—God is calling His people to get up and go take a look! He is showing us something in advance, so that we can be prepared. The world is going to change and God is giving us signs in the heavens.

Oftentimes when people talk about prophecy, they make it all about the negatives—the doom and gloom. I don't believe this is the point of prophecy. It will be bad for those who don't see what God is doing or who refuse to pay attention. While there will certainly be tough and challenging times ahead, for those of us who are looking up—with eyes to see and ears to hear—our redemption draws near. God's great end-time outpouring is at hand.

LOOK AND SEE WHAT GOD IS DOING

Let me share a powerful biblical example I taught to my church recently. Remember the beginning of Moses' story? Moses was out tending his father-in-law's flocks one day when God appeared and spoke to him from within a burning bush. This is what it says: "So he looked, and behold, the bush was burning with fire, but the bush was not consumed. Then Moses said, 'I will now turn aside and see this great sight, why the bush does not burn'" (Exodus 3:2–3).

Now watch what happened. The next verse says this: "So when the LORD saw that he turned aside to look, God called to him from the midst of the bush and said, 'Moses, Moses!'" (Exodus 3:4).

In ancient wisdom, it's taught that when Moses stopped and turned to see the burning bush, he craned his neck to take a deep, intentional look. The word "to look or see" in Hebrew, is usually *vayaar*. But when it says that Moses turned to see the burning bush, instead of using the normal Hebrew word *vayaar*, it is spelled *vaya'ar*. The difference is that God changes the spelling by adding the small Hebrew letter *yod*, that little apostrophe, which represents the presence of God.

By adding the yod, we learn a secret. The deeper meaning here is that Moses didn't just turn to see the burning bush, he purposely turned to see what God was doing. When Moses went through the extra effort to see what God was doing, he released the presence of God into his destiny. Because he was determined to look, God revealed His plans to him. He wasn't inflexible or stubborn, and definitely wasn't stiff-necked. It's what separated Moses from the crowd. This is a key reason why God chose him.

Moses craned his neck (the opposite of being stiff necked) to see what God was doing. Sometimes religion can try to make us all a little stiff necked. This is what Jesus is talking about when He says man's traditions nullify the Word of God (Mark 7:13). But when we decide to look up—crane our necks—we'll see God's "burning bush," or in this case, the eighth series of four blood moons.

Just like Moses, our most exciting journey will begin, and just like Moses and the children of Israel, the journey is taking us all to the Promised Land, back to Israel and back to Jerusalem.

I thank God that twenty something years ago the Lord spoke to me in Israel and said, "I am going to teach you to reread the Bible through the eyes of a Jewish Jesus." This was a type of burning bush experience for me. I "craned my neck" to see what God was doing, but for virtually all of the past twenty years, I was seen as a kind of a heretic.

People have respected that the Lord called Tiz and I to partner with Him to build seven churches, they've seen our ministry has been built on soul winning, they've known our message on breaking family curses has set His people free from bondages and afflictions. Our history in ministry is filled with example after example of lives that have been transformed, marriages that have been restored, businesses and financial situations that have come back from the brink, and people diagnosed with sickness and disease have received miracle healing.

Salvation sets our spirits and souls free, breaking curses sets our lives free and the seven places Jesus shed His blood releases every covenant blessing into our lives. It's been paid in full! Jewish roots opens our eyes to the truth that sets us free, and now, as we see God's signs in the heavens, these four blood moons prepares us for the greatest time in history—the latter rain—living under the open windows of heaven!

THE BLOOD MOON HISTORY: THE WORLD CHANGED FOREVER

Earlier I mentioned the seven times NASA has documented the four blood moons aligning with biblical holidays since the time of Christ. With each, world events unfolded in a remarkable way. NASA has confirmed these dates and we are able to go back into history to discover what was happening before, during, and after these times. Let me show you the previous seven blood moons and some of the historical events they correspond with:

1. 162–163 AD: Great Famine, widespread plague, and another era of overwhelming persecution of Christians begins by the Roman Empire under Marcus Aurelius

2. 795–796 AD: Charlemagne's successful campaigns ended centuries of Arab invasions into Western Europe

3. 842–843 AD: Events leading up to the Sack of Rome by the Islamic nations

4. 860–861 AD: Christian Byzantine Empire defeats Islamic armies in Turkey and stops the invasion of Eastern Europe

5. 1493–1494 AD: The Spanish Inquisition, torture, and expulsion of Jews from Spain and Columbus' expedition to the New World

6. 1949–1950 AD: Israel reborn as a nation, the Arab-Israeli War and the signing of the 1949 Armistice Agreement

7. 1967–1968 AD: Israel's Six Day War and the taking back of Jerusalem for the first time since 70 AD

As you can see, each of these seven appearances has been accompanied by world-changing events. Each of the seven four blood moon events dramatically affected and changed the world. Each of these had both huge spiritual and economic shifts. Spiritually and economically, kingdoms were turned upside down and transferred into other hands. Although a whole book could be, and I'm sure has been, written on each of these supernatural, historic events, for the sake of time let's focus on the last three. As you will see, these have changed the world. This current one will change not only history but I believe it will change your life forever!

THE FOUR BLOOD MOONS OF 1493–1494 AD

You've heard the saying, "In 1492 Columbus sailed the ocean blue." In America, we all grew up hearing that 1492 was an important date in our history. Significant as it was that Columbus "discovered" America, let's not forget the other side of this story. King Ferdinand and Queen Isabella, who ruled Spain, conspired with Pope Sixtus IV to launch the brutal Spanish Inquisition. Under the guise of maintaining the Catholic form of faith, what really followed was intense persecution of any who didn't convert to Catholicism, especially the Jews.

Although Jewish people everywhere tried to live out their faith in peace and as inconspicuously as possible, they became the prime targets of the Inquisition. Christianity had long detested and persecuted the Jews, but this time in history it went to new levels. Accusations and intolerance were rampant by both the Church and the government. Leaders in both took what can only be described as horrific actions.

Anti-Semitism flourished in cities and countries throughout Europe. Torture was regularly used to coerce confessions and force conversions to Catholicism. History records the Church sponsored everything from intimidation, beatings, confiscation of possessions and property, to thousands being burned alive at the stake—just for being Jewish.

It was in 1492 that Ferdinand and Isabella issued a decree to banish all Jewish people from Spain. Let Christopher Columbus tell you—this is how he began his famous diary: "In the same month in which their Majesties issued the edict that all Jews should be driven out of the kingdom and its territories, in the same month they gave me the order to undertake with sufficient men my expedition of discovery to the Indies."

Here's another of those things people might think is just a coincidence: the day the decree demanded Jews leave Spain was, on the Jewish calendar, the Ninth of Av (Tishah b'Av). In Jewish history, the Ninth of Av is significant—it's the day that both the first and the second Temple were destroyed.

History tells us that on their way out of Spain, the Jews were stripped of their wealth and possessions. Many scholars believe that the money taken from the Jewish people financed

Columbus' discovery of the New World. Some historians write that it was actually two wealthy and influential Jewish men who had previously helped finance many things for King Ferdinand who came and offered a huge sum of money to reverse the decree and allow the Jews to stay.

King Ferdinand was almost ready to change the edict when Torquemada, the Chief Inquisitor for the Catholic Church, confronted Ferdinand by showing a naked Jesus on a cross and saying, "If you do this, you violate Christ." At that moment, the King yielded to the pressure and forced thousands of Jews to leave Spain.

After Spain killed, tortured, forced conversions, stole property, business, and wealth, and eventually forced all Jews to leave the country, their power began to decline: economically, politically, and militarily. To this day, they have never fully recovered. Incidentally, do you know what Spain is doing right now? I read in the *Jerusalem Post* that they are asking Jews, who had ancestry back to 1492, to move back to Spain, welcoming them back with open arms and offering them an opportunity to reclaim their lost land.

It's worth mentioning that many of those same historians believe that, in regard to his voyage west, one of Columbus' personal goals was to find a safe place where Jews could live free of persecution. Some even claim Christopher Columbus was not Italian or Spanish but Jewish! History also proves the first couple letters Columbus wrote after finding the Americas were not written back to the King but were written back to the Jewish men who financed him. This leaves little doubt it was Jewish money that funded the discovery of America.

How does all of this relate? It shows the dramatic change in the world during the time of these four blood moons. King Ferdinand and Queen Isabella were head of the most politically and economically powerful country in the world. The discovery of America led to a transfer of political, economic, military, and spiritual power. Spain, on the other hand, began a rapid decline.

This is what we need to remember from Genesis 12:3, where God says, "I will bless those who bless you, and I will curse him who curses you." Today, may all of America and the rest of the world remember this promise. May we all have "eyes to see" this. Those who bless the Jewish people, which includes Israel, the land given to them by God and also by the Allied Forces after World War I, through internationally approved resolutions and mandates.

THE FOUR BLOOD MOONS OF 1949–1950 AD

Some twenty-five hundred years before the four blood moons of 1949–1950 appeared, God said this through the prophet

Ezekiel: "For I will take you from among the nations, gather you out of all countries, and bring you into your own land... Then you shall dwell in the land that I gave to your fathers; you shall be My people, and I will be your God" (Ezekiel 36:24, 28).

The tetrad of 1949–1950 signaled the fulfillment of this Scripture and many others. Talk about signs, wonders, and miracles! God's people had been scattered all over the world since 70 AD when the Roman Emperor Titus drove them out of Israel and destroyed Jerusalem. There has never been anything close to this in all of human history—a nation that lost their land, their government, their language, their identity, and then came back! Many people for many years said, "This is what proves the Bible to be false. Israel will never become a nation again. It can't happen, it won't happen." Not only did God say it will happen, He gave us four blood moons as a sign in the heavens.

This is one of the greatest of God's miracles and promises to have ever taken place—even though most people thought it could never happen. This great return of the Jews to the land of Israel happened right on the heels of World War II and the Holocaust. In May 1948, the United Nations officially gave the Jewish people their ancestral homeland and the State of Israel was legally established!

The Jewish people overcame the bitter opposition and unsuccessful invasion by the surrounding Arab nations. Despite the ongoing hostility, biblical prophecy was fulfilled, Israel was restored as a nation, and the desert began to bloom for the first time in nearly two thousand years. There was a spiritual and economic transfer of wealth—a real miracle of miracles—and it signaled the hand of God was on Israel. In 1949, the first permanent Israel government was formed and the international peace treaty was signed by Egypt, Lebanon, Jordan, and Syria.

THE FOUR BLOOD MOONS OF 1967–1968 AD

How about another miraculous moment in history? Since the day Israel was declared a sovereign state in 1948, and despite legitimate truces and treaties, tension with the Arab neighbor-states has continued without stopping. In the days leading up to the Six-Day War in 1967, Egypt, Jordan, and Syria amassed troops and tanks on the borders of Israel poised to make good on all of their threats. With half a million men and thousands of tanks and aircraft, it was way beyond what Israel could hope to muster in defense.

In just six days, however, despite the impossible odds, Israel won a great victory! In what can only be considered a major military miracle, Israel defeated the attacking Arab nations. Even though they were a decisive underdog, the Israeli

Army was able to regain control of the Gaza Strip, the Sinai Peninsula, the West Bank, and the Golan Heights with their tiny army. What is most remarkable is they regained control of Jerusalem. It had been nineteen hundred years since any Jew had been able to lay their hands on the Western Wall and pray. The Holy City was back in Jewish hands for the first time since 70 AD and the destruction of the Temple.

3

A Phenomenal Prophet
and His Incredible Prophecy!

Surely the Lord GOD does nothing, Unless He
reveals His secret to His servants the prophets. A lion
has roared! Who will not fear? The Lord GOD has
spoken! Who can but prophesy?

—Amos 3:7–8

Where I live outside of Dallas, there are hundreds of vacant acres, not a soul as far as you can see. I've been walking my dogs out there for years. There's this pile of junk I've walked by hundreds of times—it looks like somebody tore down a building and trucked all the debris out there and dumped it. I'll bet it's been there twenty years, untouched. There's not even a road to it anymore, it just sits there, abandoned.

One day, I was walking by that pile of junk, thinking about that passage I referred to earlier in Genesis 3 where Moses craned his neck to look at what God was doing. Joking with myself, I decided to crane my neck and look at that heap of rubbish.

So I bent my head around and intentionally took a good, long look. You know what? I saw a sign! A real sign—as in a seven- or-eight-foot-tall automotive sign, half-buried, but sticking up out of that pile! Now, I collect old automotive signs, oil cans, and stuff so this was a real find. I thought, *Wow! I've got to go get Tiz to help me dig that thing up and drag it home!*

Think about it, I'd been walking by this pile for years and never slowed down to take a meaningful look. Later, when Tiz and I were talking about it, she said, "It's just like the Jewish roots. The Church has been walking past it for years and considered it nothing more than a pile of junk. But in these last days we're craning our necks to take a closer look, and God is revealing mysteries that have been buried there, just waiting to be found."

As we went out to get that sign—yes, we went to get it!—we talked about Ephesians 3, where Paul talks about a mystery hidden since the beginning of time, but in these last days it's being revealed. The treasures God has stored up and kept hidden until now, just like this sign, are being discovered. It was a divine moment that really came alive in our hearts. We couldn't wait to get back home and look at our notes on Ephesians. When we got back, the Lord led us to this specific passage:

> For this reason I, Paul, the prisoner of Christ Jesus for you Gentiles—if indeed you have heard of the dispensation of the grace of God which was given to me for you, how that by revelation He made known to me the mystery [as I have briefly written already, by which, when you read, you may understand my knowledge in the mystery of Christ], which in other ages was not made known to the sons of men, as it has now been revealed by the Spirit to His holy apostles and prophets: that the Gentiles should be fellow heirs, of the same body, and partakers of His promise in Christ through the gospel, of which I became a minister according to the gift of the grace of God given to me by the effective working of His power. (Ephesians 3:1–7)

Throughout the ages, God has had a plan concerning Jews and Gentiles that He kept hidden from everyone. It has to do with the Gentiles becoming joint heirs with the Jews in everything God has promised. Unfortunately, over the centuries, both Jew and Christian lost this revelation of unity and the goal of becoming one new man. The gift of grace God gave through the Messiah has, in many ways, been squandered. It hasn't been used to advance this unique relationship between us. To earlier generations, this was a mystery, and even today it's unknown to most church people, but things are changing—changing rapidly.

We are living in a time when God is offering us an opportunity to look up and see this fundamental part of God's redemptive plan. It's an incredible time to learn many biblical secrets from our Jewish brothers that we've lost over time. As this relationship is restored, we will also see a restoration of prophetic wisdom that both will share and it will release a flood of God's glory.

A PROPHECY OF LEGENDARY PROPORTIONS

God, in his great love and grace, gives us even more prophetic signs of what is about to happen. The Lord knows the "wiles" of the Devil. He knows that the enemy will try one of the oldest tricks in the book. Sure, history changes every time these four blood moons fall on biblical holidays. Sure, there has only been seven, the biblical number of completion, since the time of Jesus. Sure, this series is number eight, a new beginning, but the enemy would have you believe this is all just a "coincidence." But as we know, there is *no* word for coincidence.

The Lord has already given us more than enough to catch our attention and open our eyes. The history of the four blood moons shows us how dramatically the world has changed through the transfer of power, wealth and spiritual leadership. Since this is so important for all of us, He gave us even more.

Let's look first at the amazing pinpoint accuracy of one of God's prophets and one of Judaism's most legendary and prolific rabbis, the Rabbi Judah ben Samuel (1140–1217). He was known as the Light of Israel in his homeland of Germany and was a very devout man of God. In 1215, he delivered a series of prophecies on the future of Judaism—all of which eventually took place exactly as the Lord showed the Rabbi.

Let me first give you the entire prophecy that Rabbi gave in 1215 and then break it down as it unfolded and you will have no doubt that this is a prophetic word for our time, for you, for the world, and, oh yes, what a "coincidence." It all is coming to a grand finale during the four blood moons. We must have eyes to see and ears to hear, as we listen to the prophetic word.

In 1215, Rabbi Judah ben Samuel prophesied that the Ottomans would rule Jerusalem for eight Jubilees (four hundred years). Then Jerusalem would change hands and power but would be called "no man's land" for one Jubilee (fifty years). After that additional Jubilee, the Jewish people would once again rule Jerusalem, and it would not be in the hands of the Gentiles anymore. Then for one more Jubilee, God would prepare the world for the coming of the Messiah. After that fifty-year period, we would enter into the Messianic Era.

Please note, he did not predict the date of the coming of the Messiah, just the Messianic Era.

The Rabbi prophesied that these Ottoman Turks would rule Jerusalem for eight Jubilees. At the time he spoke this, nobody had even heard of the Ottomans—they were known as the Osmans, a small tribe that lived in what's now modern-day Turkey. Two years later, the Rabbi died, but what he prophesied lives to this day.

For the next six Jubilees, the next three hundred years, these Ottoman Turks, these Osmans, became more and more powerful. As the story is told, Europe had trouble pronouncing the name Osman so by a fluke they started calling them Ottomans, exactly what the Rabbi had prophesied three hundred years beforehand. He was prophesying about a tribe of people that nobody had ever heard of.

In 1517, the Ottoman Turks grew very powerful and actually invaded Israel and controlled Jerusalem—and you guessed it, just as the Rabbi prophesied, they were in charge for eight Jubilees. A Jubilee year occurs every fifty years, so that equals a total of four hundred years.

The Ottoman Empire became one of the largest and longest lasting empires in history. It replaced the Byzantine Empire as the major power in the Eastern Mediterranean.

The Ottoman Empire reached its peak under Suleiman, who reigned from 1520 to 1566. It expanded to cover: Turkey, the Balkans, Hungry, Greece, Austria, Romania, Bulgaria, Macedonia, Israel (Palestine), Jordan, Lebanon, Syria, parts of Arabia, and much of the coastal strip of Northern Africa.

Now, fast forward to 1917 when during World War I, General Edmond Allenby was sent by the British Empire to remove the Turkish Empire and reestablish the nation of Israel. Allenby was a believer in Bible prophecy and as he looked upon Jerusalem, he sent a telegraph to the King of England that said: "I, in good conscience, cannot shoot a bullet into God's city."

The king sent back a telegram, which said only one thing: "Pray." They began to pray and the next day, which just happened to be the first day of Chanukah, the Festival of Lights—the miracle of rededicating the Temple—the Ottomans laid down their weapons and walked out of Jerusalem without a bullet fired. This was exactly eight jubilees, or four hundred years, later.

But there's more. The second part of Rabbi Samuel's prophesy was that although Israel would be taken, Jerusalem would be designated "no man's land" for one more Jubilee—fifty more years. Even though Jews and Arabs were both living in Jerusalem at this time, in 1917 the League of Nations officially declared the city to be "no man's land."

In April of 1920, the San Remo Conference, an international meeting, was held in Italy following the conclusion of World War I. It determined the precise boundaries for territories captured by the Allied Forces. Land that was previously under the control of the Ottoman Empire was divided by Great Britain, France, Italy, and Japan (with the USA as a neutral observer).

It was at this conference that these nations created the modern-day map of the Middle East. They passed an international mandate that created the new Arab states of Syria, Lebanon, Iraq, and Jordan. I could go on to show you much more about the treaties that were signed, how the worldwide community approved of how each of these territories were divided, and how international law says these decisions cannot be repealed.

The important thing is to see the next two points of fact and of prophecy. First, Israel was included in these divided territories and given to the British under the old Roman name of Palestine. This was now the officially reconstructed Jewish homeland, approved by the fifty-two members of the League of Nations, legally binding to this day under international law. The entire area totaled 120,466 square miles but to appease certain opponents, by July 24, 1922, the territory was reduced by 77 percent of the original mandate.

The second thing I want you to see is that not only every nation was divided by this mandate, but Jerusalem was to be "no man's land" which lasted one Jubilee just like Rabbi Judah ben Samuel prophesied seven hundred years earlier. Remember, in ancient Hebrew there is no word for coincidence.

When you do the math, 1917 plus fifty years brings us to 1967. On June 5, 1967, exactly one Jubilee later, all the Arabs troops, all the Arab nations gathered together in an act of war and attacked Israel. Historically this is known as the Six-Day War. The Arab nations had a great army of soldiers, weapons, planes, and munitions. The fledgling nation of Israel had bus drivers and schoolteachers grabbing old weapons and even resorting to machetes and shovels to fight off this act of aggression.

It must be understood that the Arab nations didn't just want to defeat Israel, they planned to make good on all their threats to wipe Israel off the face of the earth. They invaded Israel with 465,000 troops, 2,800 tanks, 800 fighter planes, and hundreds of cannons and rockets.

But by a miracle of God and according to the prophecies, Israel prevailed and all of Jerusalem was retaken. It was then, at that divine moment, that Israeli soldiers laid their hands on the Western Wall for the first time since 70 AD. No one thought these events would or could ever happen in their life-time, but fifty years and one Jubilee cycle later, Jerusalem was back in Jewish control, just as the Rabbi had predicted. Not only did he prophecy this, so did Jesus when He said in Luke 21:24 that Jerusalem will be trampled by Gentiles until the times of the Gentiles are fulfilled, or over.

Now watch what happens next. Rabbi Judah ben Samuel prophesied that after that, when the Jews again controlled Jerusalem, God would give the world one more Jubilee, a time of preparation, before the Messianic Era would begin. This begins September 23, 2015, on Yom Kippur, the Day of Atonement. This is just days before the fourth blood moon. But wait, you may be thinking, when you add fifty years to 1967, it doesn't come out to 2015, it comes out to 2017.

This is important you understand what I'm about to show you. According to rabbinical teaching, when we are in the will of God and are in control of Jerusalem, God counts time using the biblical calendar. So now, since the Jews have retaken Jerusalem, God's timetable no longer goes by the world's calendar of 365 days per year. We revert back to the biblical calendar, which is based on the moon and not the sun, so there are 360 days in a year—not 365. And 360 days a year from June 7, 1967, leads us exactly to the moment on September 23, 2015—Jubilee!

During this period from 1967 to the next Jubilee, which begins on September 23, 2015, God is giving the world a chance to prepare for the coming of the Messiah. He is revealing things to His prophets, who in turn are revealing them to the Church and to the world. During 2015, we will experience the eighth in the series of four blood moons since the times of Christ. God is shouting to nations that this is the new beginning we've all been waiting for! May we all have eyes to see and ears to hear!

4

The Miracle of Shemittah and Jubilee

You will arise and have mercy on Zion; for the time to
favor her, yes, the set time, has come.

—Psalm 102:13

So far we have taken a profound look at the signs in the heavens, prophecies of God and man, but now I want to show
you how all of these tie in with His appointed times and the
prophesy He wants to release into your life.

Look with me at God's Word written by Paul to the Church
in Ephesians 5:25–27:

Husbands, love your wives, just as Christ also loved the
church and gave Himself for her, that He might sanc-
tify and cleanse her with the washing of water by the
word, that He might present her to Himself a glorious

church, not having spot or wrinkle or any such thing,
but that she should be holy and without blemish.

In studying God's Word, you have to understand that everything the Lord says to us has two sides, the heavenly and
the earthly or the spiritual and the physical. We can see this
in what the Lord is showing us in Ephesians, "Husbands, love
your wives as Christ loves the Church." Jesus doesn't just love
us, in that He died for our sins to make heaven our home,
that's the spiritual. Just as a husband is to do: He provides for
us, protects us, and gives us a life more abundantly.

Verse 27 says He is coming for a glorious Church, not having spot or wrinkle. Let's look at the spiritual part of that. He
is coming for a holy Church—a clean Church (no spot). He is
coming for a loving Church (no wrinkle). They will know you
are my disciple, that you have love for one another.

Now let's look at the physical, or earthly, part of this teaching. No spot or wrinkle—no debt, no sickness. Paul says this
will come about by the "washing of water by the Word." The
water, or what is known as the *mikvah*, breaks all contact with
failure. In the last days, God's Word will come alive (*rhema*)
and through the truth we know and understand, we will be set
free. God said you are to be the head and not the tail. You are
to be above only and not beneath. You are to be the lender and
not the borrower.

THE SECRETS ON GOD'S DIVINE CALENDAR

Now, let me show you what has for a long time been a mystery to much of the world. In the end times, God promises to "open the eyes of the Gentiles."

Most of us have heard of the "Year of Jubilee." The Bible teaches that Jubilee is one of God's great appointed times. Jubilee is when God supernaturally cancels debts, sets captives free, returns what has been lost. It is a time, an appointed time, to expect great miracles from God's hand.

The name *Jubilee* is from the Hebrew word *yovel*, which means "ram's horn." The ram's horn or shofar is God's trumpet. Throughout biblical times and even today, the shofar is sounded to announce many important things. For one, it is a call to war. It also announces the coronation of the king. It is also used as an annual wake-up call to return to God during the forty-day period leading up to the High Holy Days of Rosh Hashanah and Yom Kippur, the Day of Atonement—which just happens to be the official start date for Jubilee.

Look at Psalm 102:13: "You will arise and have mercy on Zion; For the time to favor her, Yes, the set time, has come." This time when you read it, instead of "Zion," put your name there, and insert your name in place of "her." "You will arise and have mercy on (your name); For the time to favor (your name), Yes, the set time, has come."

Jubilee is the set time, the appointed time, but if we have eyes to see we don't have to wait. We can "look up" at the four blood moons. If we have "ears to hear" the prophecies given to us, we can walk in that Jubilee blessing right now. The secret is found in the teaching of Shemittah. Let me explain.

Many times the Church has not taught on the feasts because it has said, "These are Jewish Feasts." But God says in Leviticus 23, "These are the Feasts of the Lord." What you need to know is that before you enter into Jubilee, you first have to have a year of Shemittah. The current Shemittah began on September 24, 2014, and ends September 22, 2015, the day before Jubilee.

Let me show you how it works. First take a look at Leviticus 25:1–4, 8–13 and 20–21:

> And the LORD spoke to Moses on Mount Sinai, saying, "Speak to the children of Israel, and say to them: 'When you come into the land which I give you, then the land shall keep a sabbath to the LORD. Six years you shall sow your field, and six years you shall prune your vineyard, and gather its fruit; but in the seventh year

there shall be a sabbath of solemn rest for the land, a sabbath to the Lord. You shall neither sow your field nor prune your vineyard. (Leviticus 25:1–4)

And you shall count seven sabbaths of years for yourself, seven times seven years; and the time of the seven sabbaths of years shall be to you forty-nine years. Then you shall cause the trumpet of the Jubilee to sound on the tenth day of the seventh month; on the Day of Atonement you shall make the trumpet to sound throughout all your land. And you shall consecrate the fiftieth year, and proclaim liberty throughout all the land to all its inhabitants. It shall be a Jubilee for you; and each of you shall return to his possession, and each of you shall return to his family. That fiftieth year shall be a Jubilee to you; in it you shall neither sow nor reap what grows of its own accord, nor gather the grapes of your untended vine. For it is the Jubilee; it shall be holy to you; you shall eat its produce from the field. 'In this Year of Jubilee, each of you shall return to his possession. (Leviticus 25 8–13)

And if you say, "What shall we eat in the seventh year, since we shall not sow nor gather in our produce?" Then I will command My blessing on you in the sixth year, and it will bring forth produce enough for three years. (Leviticus 25:20–21)

- First: God says every seventh year will be Sabbath year.
- Second: On that seventh, Sabbath, year; you are not to sow, nor prune. (Keep in mind, this is only to physically take place in the land of Israel itself.)

Now, why did God tell them that? The answer is found in Deuteronomy 8. When you get a chance, read the whole chapter, it is an amazing teaching. God tells us if we follow what He says, we will be abundantly blessed. In verses 7–8, He describes a good land of abundance, in every way. It says we will lack nothing. This is a prophecy and the promise of the abundant life the Lord has for you and me. It's a life of "good measure, pressed down, shaken together and overflowing." A life where "everything we put our hand to God will cause to prosper." A life where "every place we put the soul of our feet He will give it to us as an inheritance." A land—a life—where "we are more than conquerors." What a great word! How can we go wrong?

Then comes the "but." In verse 10, God warns us that the real danger comes not when we have needs, but when we are "full"—when all our needs are met. He tells us to make sure that we "bless the Lord." I can't help but thinking about all of us sitting down at a meal and saying grace before we eat. We are thanking God for His provision in our lives. We are hungry, but before we eat, we give thanks, we "bless the Lord." But, do you know that ancient Bible wisdom tells us to thank the Lord after we eat? This is just as important, if not more important, to do now that we have eaten are "full."

This warning continues in verse 11–13: "Don't forget the Lord…when you have eaten and are full," i.e., living in beautiful homes, businesses are flourishing, and economy is strong. Verses 17–19: "Then you say in your heart, 'My power and the might of my hand have gained me this wealth.' And you shall remember the LORD your God, for it is He who gives you power to get wealth that He may establish His covenant which He swore to your fathers, as it is this day. Then it shall be, if you by any means forget the LORD your God, and follow other gods, and serve them and worship them, I testify against you this day that you shall surely perish."

This is God's reason for Shemittah every seven years and especially the final Shemittah just before Jubilee. God's concern is that He knows us too well. He knows that when we are in need, we call on Him to help, but He also knows that it is very easy to forget. It's so easy to think everything we enjoy came through our own efforts. All—and I mean all—of our blessings come from Him. Not only is He "the same yesterday, today and tomorrow," but unfortunately so are we, but that can change.

SHEMITTAH AND ISRAEL'S SEVENTY YEARS OF CAPTIVITY

The Bible says, "As a bird flies to its nest, a curse without cause cannot come." Why did God allow Israel to be defeated? Why would they be in captivity for exactly seventy years? Look at what the Lord said in 2 Chronicles 36:15-21:

"And the Lord God of their fathers sent warnings to them by His messengers, rising up early and sending them, because He had compassion on His people and on His dwelling place. But they mocked the messengers of God, despised His words, and scoffed at His prophets, until the wrath of the Lord arose against His people, till there was no remedy. Therefore He brought against them the king of the Chaldeans, who killed their young men with the sword in the house of their sanctuary, and had no compassion on young man or virgin, on the aged or the weak; He gave them all into his hand. And all the articles from the house of God, great and small, the treasures of the house of the Lord, and the treasures of the king and of his leaders, all these he took to Babylon. Then they burned the house of God, broke down the wall of Jerusalem, burned all its palaces with fire, and destroyed all its precious possessions. And those who escaped from the sword he carried away to Babylon, where they became servants to him and his sons until the rule of the kingdom of Persia, to fulfill the word of the Lord by the mouth of Jeremiah, until the land had enjoyed her Sabbaths. As long as she lay desolate she kept Sabbath, to fulfill seventy years" (See also Jeremiah 25:1-14 and 29:10).

Why exactly seventy years? Again we must be like Moses and "crane our necks" to see what God is doing. The exact number seventy is for every year that Israel did not keep Shemittah. Or, to say it plainly, they didn't feel like they had to rely on God anymore. They were full, they lived in nice houses, their jobs, businesses, and economy were flourishing, and they forgot "it was the Lord Who gave them power to gain wealth."

Sound like anybody—any nation—we know? Let me just speak about America. We are at the door of exactly what happened to Israel and Babylon, but it's not too late. Some of us have forgotten it is the Lord Who has blessed our nation. Some of us have forgotten what our Founding Fathers didn't want us to forget—we are One Nation Under God. This was so important to them they even put "In God We Trust" on our money—a powerful reminder not to trust in our own ability, in our own "might and strength," but by His Spirit. Some have forgotten to the point that we can't pray in public anymore, or display the Ten Commandments in public places and government buildings.

Shemittah is not just about a year, but it is for us to remember it is the Lord our God who gives us power to gain wealth—to prosper. It's God—the God of Abraham, Isaac, and Jacob who blesses our nation, our families, our economy— our everything. This is what Moses is reminding Israel (and us today) in Deuteronomy 8:18 states: "And you shall remember the LORD your God, for it is He who gives you power to get wealth, that He may establish His covenant which He swore to your fathers, as it is this day."

A HISTORY LESSON OF TRUTH THAT WILL SET YOU FREE

Almost every Christian in the world has heard at least one sermon from the book of Malachi. In fact, as soon as the pastor says, "Let's turn to the book of Malachi," we all think of tithes and offerings. I have heard, more than once, a preacher insist that "there is nothing for us in the Old Testament" and yet will preach on tithes and offerings. Ha! Right! Yet, when we teach on "a tenth is the Lord's and offerings besides," in reality, most of us have never been taught what that really means.

Remember that Israel went into Babylonian captivity for seventy years because they did not keep the seventh Sabbath year called the Shemittah. Once again, the important thing to see, to learn, is they felt like they didn't need to rely on God anymore. They forgot "it was Him who gave power" in all things: to gain wealth, to get rain, to defeat sickness, to be victorious over every enemy. So for every year they acted this way, they became slaves to their enemy. Seventy Shemittahs—seventy years in captivity.

But God moved on behalf of His people. Instead of death at the end of the seventy-year period, they were released with blessings to return to Jerusalem to rebuild the Temple and the city. As soon as they returned to Jerusalem, there was a meeting that took place called "the Great Assembly," in Hebrew *Anshei Knesset HaGedolah*. This was such an important time in history, that even today the Israeli Senate in Jerusalem is called "The Knesset."

At this Great Assembly were 120 scribes, sages, and prophets. Among those in attendance were Ezra, Nehemiah, Mordechai, Nahum, Haggai, Zechariah, and Malachi. They gathered together because they were tired of their enemies having power over them. They were tired of fear, poverty, hunger, and death. So they asked God to tell them what to do and the Lord answered through Malachi:

> "For I am the LORD, I do not change; therefore you are not consumed, O sons of Jacob. Yet from the days of your fathers you have gone away from My ordinances and have not kept them. Return to Me, and I will return to you," says the LORD of hosts. "But you said, 'In what way shall we return?' Will a man rob God? Yet you have robbed Me! But you say, 'In what way have we robbed You?' In tithes and offerings. You are cursed with a curse, for you have robbed Me, even this whole nation. Bring all the tithes into the storehouse,

that there may be food in My house, and try Me now in this," says the LORD of hosts, "If I will not open for you the windows of heaven and pour out for you such blessing that there will not be room enough to receive it." (Malachi 3:6–10)

This was said at the very end of Israel's seventy years of captivity. Here is an amazing quote from a great book of Jewish wisdom-Ethics of the Fathers. "Exile comes upon the world on account of idolatry, sexual immorality, murder, and the failure to observe the Shemittah" (Pirkei Avot 5:11).

So the teaching is, every people and every nation that forgets Shemittah, that forgets it is God we are to trust, will experience some type of destruction. Understand that exile involves more than just being separated from the land, it also involves living in a state of fear, a broken state of being, doubt, and disempowerment.

This makes me think of America right now. We have allowed too many of our politicians and celebrities and sadly some of our religious leaders to take God off the throne. Many of you in other countries are seeing the same results, "a broken state of being." Homes, families, and lives are being torn apart. Divorce is an epidemic. Children are running wild—we all know the stats.

Doubt and living in a state of fear means no one knows what's going to happen next. Will a building collapse because of a religious fanatic? Will our schools collapse because education isn't important anymore? Will our economy collapse because our politicians are telling us the government will take care of everything? So now we vote for a living, instead of work for a living. Is the Lord Jehovah Jireh, our Provider, or is the government now our provider?

Disempowerment is seen by the fact that America is losing its power all over the world. I also see so many other nations that lost their power years ago. Nations and countries that were great when God was the Great Almighty and still on the throne.

IT'S NOT TOO LATE—THE BEST IS YET TO COME!

I know with a 100 percent certainty that it is not too late for any of us. That is why the Lord is shouting to us with the four blood moons, with the voice of the prophets, with the Shemittah year leading into the year of Jubilee and with the exact time of God fulfilling His Word. Now what I'm about to show you next is so very important. Let's go back to Malachi 3 where God gives Israel the answer on how to stay out of captivity. He says, "Return to Me, and I will return unto you."

God calls for His people to return (*teshuvah*) every year at *Rosh Hashanah*—the head of the year. Now let God open your eyes that you may "see" a great appointed time He has set for the world! The word *return* has a far-reaching biblical impact: repentance of sin, a spiritual awakening to reconnect yourself to God and His Word, to prayer, to study, to acts of kindness, to loving your brother, to loving the stranger, to your family, to positive words, deeds, and actions. Any one of these things, every one of these things, is important to God, and the absence of any one of these opens the door to the enemy.

When God answers, "Return unto me says the Lord of Host." If you return to Him (it's your move), Jehovah Jireh, Jehovah Shalom, Jehovah Rophe, etc., will return unto you. They could remember the story of Moses speaking to God at the burning bush. "Lord, what shall I tell them your name is?" Are you the God of healing, or maybe the God of victory? Of peace? Of joy? God tells Moses, "Tell them I Am that I Am." I will be whatever you need Me to be, whenever you need Me to be it. I Am the great I Am.

Imagine their great joy? God has, in His great mercy, forgiven them and if they return unto Him, all that He is, "the great I Am" will return unto them. So, the word return, or "teshuvah," encompasses all this and more. At first God's answer may seem a bit of a surprise. "Return to Me" in tithes and offerings? Why did God choose tithes and offerings instead of all the other things that seem more spiritual or more holy?

Remember, the reason their enemies defeated Israel is that they felt they didn't need Shemittah any longer. They didn't need to rely on God. The land was flowing with milk and honey. Their crops brought a harvest and their cattle were fat. There was no enemy that couldn't be defeated. They might have said, "We don't need prayer in school or at the ball games. We don't need the Ten Commandments on school or government walls, it might offend our Babylonian neighbors."

They forgot seventy Shemittahs and as a result were taken captive by their enemies for seventy years. This is why God said the tithe—the 10 percent—belongs to God. He shows us, by putting Him first, He becomes the "Lord of our Harvest" and we live higher and better with His blessing on the 90 percent than we could ever come close to on 100 percent without His blessing. The 10 percent we cut off is a form of cutting the covenant with God.

The offering besides are the First Fruits—"three times a year we come before the Lord, and we don't come empty handed." Now watch this closely: Every year, at Rosh Hashanah, God calls for all His children to teshuvah—to return—for forty days leading up to the High Holidays. The trumpet, or *shofar*, is blown every day to sound the alarm. This is to wake up our soul because God doesn't want us to miss out on any of the blessings that are about to come our way—if we are awake, if we have "eyes to see," if we have "ears to hear."

One more time, with Rosh Hashanah, we are to wake up because God opens "the Book of Life" or "the Book of Blessing" to determine how much reward will come your way for the next year. Then, on Yom Kippur, God closes the Book and seals your blessing so that no one or nothing can steal it away from you. This promise goes even further, He not only "opens the windows of Heaven" but also "rebukes the devourer."

> Bring all the tithes into the storehouse, that there may be food in My house, and try Me now in this," says the LORD of hosts, "If I will not open for you the windows of heaven and pour out for you such blessing that there will not be room enough to receive it. "And I will rebuke the devourer for your sakes, so that he will not destroy the fruit of your ground, nor shall the vine fail to bear fruit for you in the field," says the LORD of hosts. (Malachi 3:10–11)

So let me review the dates for you. The current Shemittah year began September 24, 2014, on the first day of Rosh Hashanah. Shemittah ends on September 22, 2015. The very next day, September 23, 2015, is the last day of Yom Kippur, the day God seals your blessing. This is also the first day of the year of Jubilee. You may not hear the shofar blowing, but you can look up and see the four blood moons, you can listen and hear the words of God's prophets, you can awaken your soul and rejoice—for the best is yet to come. Our redemption draws near, praise the Lord!

Then a few days later, on September 28, 2015, comes the last of the four blood moons. Remember, this is no coincidence. If you are reading this book—even after the four blood moons have come and gone—it's not too late to get in on God's great blessings. Trust me when I say the Lord Jesus wants you to open your eyes to the truth, to trust in God—the God of Abraham, Isaac, and Jacob.

It's amazing that as I am writing this, friends of mine in Israel tell me that the whole of the land is preparing for Shemittah. They may be surrounded by enemies, you may be surrounded by enemies, but if God is for you—who can be against you? The word Shemittah means release. Let God release you from "Babylon," from slavery, from exile, from lack, from want, from bondage and limitations.

5

The Wake-Up Call: Sounding the Alarm!

Blow the trumpet in Zion, and sound an alarm in My holy mountain! Let all the inhabitants of the land tremble; for the day of the LORD is coming, For it is at hand.

—Joel 2:1

How many of us have missed something important because we slept too long? Maybe it was a flight we neglected to catch or an appointment we needed to keep. We all know that panicked feeling when our eyes open, we look at the clock, and reality hits us. We missed it. Maybe the alarm didn't go off. Maybe we forgot to set the alarm, didn't hear it, or pushed the snooze button once too many times. For whatever reason, we miss the appointment. As bad as it feels to miss an appointment with a boss, an airplane, or a doctor, just think if God made an appointment with you and you missed that one. Wow, that's what God is saying to us in Joel 2:1: "Blow the trumpet in Zion, and sound an alarm."

This is Rosh Hashanah, the Feast of Trumpets. God is saying that this time, this appointment, is so important that I don't want anybody to miss it. So blow the trumpet, sound the alarm. In ancient Israel, a trumpet, or shofar (ram's horn), was blown for two main purposes. One was to call the people to an important gathering, an assembly to meet with the Presence of the Lord. The second was to gather God's Army, for God's people to go to war and to defeat the enemy.

Each year on the Hebrew calendar, there is a forty-day period that begins in the final month of Elul. This is thirty days before Rosh Hashanah begins on Tishrei 1. During this entire period, the shofar (trumpet) is blown, the "alarm" is sounded. It is a wake-up call to rise out of our slumber.

During this forty-day period, the alarm reminds us to check our relationships: first with God and then with all others. This is what Jesus was saying, "Love God and love your neighbors." The high priest would blow the trumpet from the Temple in Jerusalem. The sound would echo off the mountain and down the valley. I've read that when men heard the alarm, they would grab a shofar and blow it, to sound the alarm to others further away from Jerusalem. They even would blow it into caves and tunnels so no one would miss the appointment God had for them, but they needed to have "ears to hear." This is one of the saddest things, I think, Jesus felt when He said they have eyes, but don't see and ears, but don't hear (Matthew 13:17).

The blowing of the trumpet, the alarm, is once again a sign of God's great love toward us. An alarm that says, "If we return to Him, He will return to us." But, I am afraid many in the last few years have "slept" through God's alarm and have missed their appointments with Him. Let's go back to the last two Shemittahs when these alarms went off.

THE SHEMITTAH ALARM ON SEPTEMBER 11, 2001

Any one of us who see and hear that date remembers the enemy attacking us. September 11, 2001, was the start of a Shemittah year. The four blood moons, once again, are signs in the heavens, miracles in the sky. They are alarms that we cannot afford to miss. I think America has gotten too prideful. I feel we are saying, "God, we have forgotten it is You who has given us power to gain wealth. They have taken You out of our schools and we did nothing. They have taken Your Ten Commandments off our walls and we said nothing." We began to think, maybe Wall Street, our own power, has given us wealth and strength to enjoy. The terrorists hit Wall Street and the World Trade Center. They hit the Pentagon, the headquarters for our military. They were coming for the Capitol until those brave souls brought down the plane.

Not only did these planes tear down buildings, they destroyed innocent lives and families who feel the pain to this day. But along with all of that tragedy, our economy crashed as well, affecting the whole world. Remember the days that followed. People were living in fear. There was doubt, uncertainty, and anxiety just as the prophets of God told us would happen if we "forgot Him and served other gods." Let me show you again:

1. In the Ethics of the Fathers, it explains that exile comes into the world on account of not keeping the Shemittah of the land…It creates a broken state of being, doubt, disempowerment, living in a state of fear.
2. The Bible teaches that to observe Shemittah guarantees abundance and blessing—to ignore it leads to judgment.

Let me once again say, God is not telling us to quit our jobs or shut down our business for the seventh Sabbath year. He is telling us as individuals and as a nation, "Put me back on the throne." The warning of Deuteronomy 8 is: "When you live in beautiful houses, your herds and flocks multiply and all you have multiplies, DO NOT FORGET IT IS THE LORD WHO GIVES YOU POWER."

When we forget the Lord, the enemy has an open door. 9/11 should have been a great wake-up call. We should have fallen on our knees and called out for repentance. We should have "returned (teshuvah)" unto God. He would have, in all His glory and power, returned to us. You know, we did for a while. If you remember, everybody was praying, going to church, and even quoting God's Word. Unfortunately, it didn't last for long. In fact, if you remember words spoken by politicians at Ground Zero referring to Isaiah 9:10 that America will rebuild and emerge stronger than ever. We will replace broken bricks of our ruin with finished stone and replant the fallen sycamore-fig tree with cedar.

These were great and powerful words, but we forgot to add the last part of verse 9: "Who say in pride and arrogance of heart." We are but tools in the Hands of God, it's not us who will rebuild, but Him. It is not us who will replace the broken bricks and replant the sycamore tree, but Him. He will do it. He will use us, if we learn, if we hear the alarm and return to Him.

SHEMITTAH 2008—AGAIN THE ALARM SOUNDS

Let me now ask you a question. After 9/11, did we wake up? When I say *we*, I don't mean just America, the US, but all of us. Every country, every government. Did we hear the alarm? Did we have eyes to see and ears to hear God calling us to return to Him? Let me be clear here. I don't believe God is the One Who did these things on 9/11. It is the Devil who comes to steal, kill, and destroy. When we, as individuals or as a nation, tell God to go away; it is an open door for the Devil to do what the Devil does, "steal, kill, and destroy."

Shemittah came again, and again God called us to return to Him in 2008, seven years later. This time as the Sabbath-Shemittah year began our economy crashed. Not only did it crash, again, this crash was one of the worst in history. Now, remember, in ancient Hebrew, there is no word for coincidence. So what I'm about to show you is a sign from God. Not only did our economy collapse, and at the time of this writing it is still in collapse, but it collapsed 777 points in one day. It is considered by economists as the worst financial crisis since the Great Depression. It was felt around the world. Banks and businesses failed, homes were foreclosed on, there was a massive loss of income, investments, jobs, and a major loss of confidence and trust.

LET'S MAKE SURE HISTORY DOESN'T REPEAT ITSELF

As I'm writing this book, the next Shemittah year is right around the corner. Once again, you may be reading this five years after I wrote it. If the Lord hasn't returned, then it's not too late for you! Return to Him. Put Him on the throne of your life. As I said, the next Shemittah year will begin during the Feast of Trumpets, September 24, 2014. This is Rosh

Hashanah, the head of the New Year. What God has in store for us is exciting. I don't believe God tells us to look at the four blood moons because He has prepared for us nothing but doom and gloom. Jesus tells us to look up to "have eyes to see," "to lift up our head," to "rejoice in the Lord" because our "redemption draws near."

The final and complete redemption is obviously the coming of the Lord, the rapture of the Church. The Messiah setting up to rule right in Jerusalem forever. I do believe the Great Redemption is near—very near—in our lifetime. Someday, may it be soon, we will hear that trumpet in the sky. Until that day, let God sound His alarm. Let Him blow the trumpet and warn all of us to put God back on the throne of our lives.

Remember, following this current Shemitah year, instead of just starting a new year, this time we start the year of Jubilee. During this Jubilee year, we have the last of the four blood moons, on the Feast of Tabernacles in 2015. This is the eighth set, a new beginning. You may ask, "Larry, when do you think the Lord will return?" I don't know, nobody does. What I do know, is this: He promised that if we returned to Him, that He, in all His glory, would return to us, to prepare a glorious bride "without spot or blemish."

6

Prosperity, Tzedakah, and Repairing a Broken World

Give, and it will be given to you: good measure,
pressed down, shaken together, and running over will
be put into your bosom. For with the same measure
that you use, it will be measured back to you.

—Luke 6:38

This next part of the book, I would like to show you how to partner with God, so that your blessings continue to grow and grow "good measure, pressed down and shaken together." Here's how: as I said earlier in this book, there has been seven series of four blood moons since the time of Jesus. The number seven symbolizes the completed purpose of God. This next tetrad of blood moons is number eight, which symbolizes man's ability to transcend the limitations of physical existence—to live above the natural.

In other words, we are about to enter into the supernatural blessings of God as never before.

As we've seen, each time the four blood moons appear, the world changed.

1. America was discovered.
2. Israel became a nation.
3. Jerusalem was back in the hands of the Jewish people.

This is what I want you to understand: The beginning of the miracle was good, but it wasn't the best. America was a wilderness. It grew and grew to become a great nation. Israel was, for the most part, a desert—dry and lifeless. Today, the desert literally blooms: great cities of business, life, communications, etc. It is a world leader in the high-tech industry. Jerusalem was mostly barren, now the world comes there to pray: Jews, Muslim, Christian—all faiths are welcome. In other words, their best was and is yet to come, and your best is yet to come.

Shemittah, putting God first, is not a ritual once every seven years but a lifestyle we can enjoy every day. The more I've studied this, the more I've come to appreciate that God gives every one of His commandments to teach us how to love Him and how to love people. In fact, the principle of Shemittah is meant to develop a dimension of compassion for others. When God gave the Shemittah laws, He connected them with *tzedakah* and being a blessing to others. Tzedakah, as we've learned, are those acts of kindness and charity we do to share the love of God with others. Here is more of the Shemittah teaching out of Leviticus 25:

> If one of your brethren becomes poor, and falls into poverty among you, then you shall help him, like a stranger or a sojourner, that he may live with you. Take no usury or interest from him; but fear your God, that your brother may live with you. You shall not lend him your money for usury, nor lend him your food at a profit. I am the LORD your God, who brought you out of the land of Egypt, to give you the land of Canaan and to be your God. (Leviticus 25:35–38)

Jesus Himself said it when He gave one of the most important teachings in the Bible, Matthew 22:36–40:

> "Teacher, which is the great commandment in the law?" Jesus said to him, "'You shall love the LORD your God with all your heart, with all your soul, and with all your mind.' This is the first and great commandment. And the second is like it: 'You shall love your neighbor as yourself.' On these two commandments hang all the Law and the Prophets."

What is the greatest commandment in all the Torah or biblical "law"? What would you say? What would I say? Probably the same thing. To love the Lord our God with all our heart, with all our soul, and with all our mind, or spirit. But, Jesus reveals a great truth that all of God's blessings rest upon not just loving God, but loving our neighbor also. Loving people, Jesus said, is equal to loving God. Let me say that again. Jesus said loving God and loving people are the same.

Look at 1 John 4:20–21: "If someone says, 'I love God,' and hates his brother, he is a liar; for he who does not love his brother whom he has seen, how can he love God whom he has not seen? And this commandment we have from Him: that he who loves God must love his brother also."

Also in John 13:34–35: "A new commandment I give to you, that you love one another; as I have loved you, that you also love one another. By this all will know that you are My disciples, if you have love for one another."

The phrase *new commandment* means a fresh commandment. When Jesus talks about a "new" covenant, He wasn't giving us a different covenant than He gave Abraham. The Bible says now that we are in Christ we are Abraham's seed (Galatians 3:29). God gave Moses the Ten Commandments which still apply today.

Sometimes religion can make people mean. Have you ever met a mean Christian—a mean "Christ-like" person? After all, that's what Christian means, to be like Christ. The world has to stop hating people in the Name of God. If we hate, we don't know God. It doesn't matter what we call ourselves or what part of the world we live in. Hate and God can't live in the same house. We pray for a "sinner," we don't hate a "sinner." For God so loved the world that He gave His only begotten Son.

REPAIRING A BROKEN WORLD

Here is the key to the growing of your blessing. Ancient Jewish wisdom tells us that the moment we were conceived, our souls stood before God. At that point, God gave every one of us a mission to *tikkun olam*, to "repair the world." God says the world is a broken place, go to the earth, and repair it.

This is what Jesus is talking about in Matthew 5:13–16:

> You are the salt of the earth; but if the salt loses its flavor, how shall it be seasoned? It is then good for nothing but to be thrown out and trampled underfoot by men. "You are the light of the world. A city that is set on a hill cannot be hidden. Nor do they light a lamp and put it under a basket, but on a lampstand, and it

gives light to all who are in the house. Let your light so shine before men, that they may see your good works and glorify your Father in heaven.

Jesus said, "You are the light of the world." What an honor that is, for we know He is truly the Light, but He also said in John 20:21, "So Jesus said to them again, 'Peace to you! As the Father has sent Me, I also send you.'" Think about that for a moment. Jesus is the Light that draws us to the throne of God and now He says you are the light. Matthew 5:16 says, "Let your light so shine before men, that they may see your good works and glorify your Father in heaven."

This is what changes us into that "Glorious Church" I wrote about earlier in this book—a Church living for God and loving people. Look at the words of Jesus concerning His reward in Matthew 25:31–40:

When the Son of Man comes in His glory, and all the holy angels with Him, then He will sit on the throne of His glory. All the nations will be gathered before Him, and He will separate them one from another, as a shepherd divides his sheep from the goats. And He will set the sheep on His right hand, but the goats on the left. Then the King will say to those on His right hand, "Come, you blessed of My Father, inherit the kingdom prepared for you from the foundation of the world: for

I was hungry and you gave Me food; I was thirsty and you gave Me drink; I was a stranger and you took Me in; I was naked and you clothed Me; I was sick and you visited Me; I was in prison and you came to Me." Then the righteous will answer Him, saying, "Lord, when did we see You hungry and feed You, or thirsty and give You drink? When did we see You a stranger and take You in, or naked and clothe You? Or when did we see You sick, or in prison, and come to You?" And the King will answer and say to them, "Assuredly, I say to you, inasmuch as you did it to one of the least of these My brethren, you did it to Me."

When we are kind to others, caring about meeting their needs, we quicken the coming of the Messiah—it is tikkun olam, repairing the world. It is seen as tipping the scales. One of the things that I love to collect are tipping scales, like we see with the "Scales of Justice." I have them in my home and at my office. I look for them to collect whenever I can. I love when people ask, "Why the scales?" Because we are weighed in the balances.

Ancient Jewish wisdom also says one day somebody will do one more act of kindness and the scales in Heaven will tip. The Father will say to His Son, "The earth has been healed, the breach repaired. Go my Son. The world is ready for their Messiah." Tikkun olam is repairing a broken world. It is preparing the world for the Messiah. It is preparing the Church to be the Glorious Bride.

THE SECRET TO THIRTY, SIXTY, HUNDREDFOLD

> But other seed fell on good ground and yielded a crop
> that sprang up, increased and produced: some thirty-
> fold, some sixty, and some a hundred.
>
> —Mark 4:8

We all have heard the teaching that the Lord gave us in Mark and once again he follows this teaching with "let him who has ears to hear let him hear." The word *hear* means more than hearing the sound of God's instruction, it means understanding what he is telling us. When Jesus says thirty, sixty, hundredfold, he didn't just pull those numbers randomly out of the air. Remember, Jesus was a Jew—a Rabbi who knew God's Word, the Torah. He was talking to other Jews who also knew the Torah. Thirty, sixty, hundredfold in Judaism has very important meanings:

1. It has to do with Deuteronomy 16:16: "Three times a year all your males shall appear before the LORD your God in the place which He chooses: at the Feast of Unleavened Bread, at the Feast of Weeks, and at the

Feast of Tabernacles; and they shall not appear before the LORD empty-handed."

Three times a year, we are to bring a special offering to the Lord. These are the First Fruit offerings that bring about a special and different kind of blessing. When we come before the Lord with all three, it releases the thirty, sixty, hundredfold blessing. Passover is the first of these which brings the thirtyfold. Pentecost (Shavuot) brings us to the sixtyfold. The Feast of Tabernacles, Sukkot, brings us to the hundredfold.

2. There is even more to the miracle of thirty, sixty, hundredfold. There are three types of giving that God instructs us to participate in. Tithes brings us to thirtyfold. Sowing our First Fruits brings us to sixtyfold. Finally, the acts of charity (tzedakah) brings us to hundredfold.

This is a very important teaching. Look with me at what Jesus is saying in Matthew 6:31–33: "Therefore do not worry, saying, 'What shall we eat?' or 'What shall we drink?' or 'What shall we wear?' For after all these things the Gentiles seek. For your heavenly Father knows that you need all these things. But seek first the kingdom of God and His righteousness, and all these things shall be added to you."

We are not to "worry about anything." Don't worry about what you will eat or what you will wear. In verse 32, He tells us two very important things. First, He says, "These are things Gentiles, those who are not in covenant with Me, have to worry about." Second, Jesus says that He knows we have need of these things. Wow, we have a blood covenant with Him. When we do our part and Jesus does His part. It could not be easier, because right here Jesus tells us what our part is: "But seek first the kingdom of God and His righteousness, and all these things shall be added to you."

Don't worry, I have a blood covenant with you. Don't worry, I know you have need of all these things. So here is what you need to do to connect with "all these things." Don't spend your energy and time "seeking" things but instead "seek" first the Kingdom of God. Seek what God is doing—seek after the Will of God. That's first.

Then the next step is to seek "His righteousness." Look first at the Hebrew word *seek*. As found in Psalm 105:4, "Seek the LORD and His strength; Seek His face evermore!" There are two different Hebrew words for *seek* used here. The first word, *darash*, means to inquire, or search carefully for something. When Tiz and I need God to give us personally or the church ministry a financial miracle, we will always begin to pray for the Lord to show us something that He is doing and how we can be part of it. "Seek-first the Kingdom of God." A great prayer is every day, "Lord, what is it you are doing and how can we partner with you in it?"

The second word for seek is *bakash*, which means "to request something desired." Let me give you a great secret, when God is getting ready to bless you, He first gives you an opportunity to be a blessing! Jesus says in Matthew 6:33, "Seek His righteousness." The word righteousness in Hebrew is the word *tzedakah*, or acts of charity, acts of kindness. Remember that our mission in life is to tikkun olam, to repair a broken world.

As I am writing this book, we are just a few months away from moving into our new Church. When we knew that we needed a financial miracle to build a new church, we began to pray for the Lord to show us what He was doing and how we could be a part of it. We were led to help feed children in Haiti right after the 2010 earthquake. That led us to build an orphanage which led to us building a second orphanage, which led us to building a school in the Dominican Republic. We also went on a "seeking" trip to Israel, which led to helping a hospital in Haifa, helping a school for very needy children, and helping many Holocaust survivors living in Israel.

One other point. When we do "charity," not only does the Lord open the window of Heaven, but He, and only God can do this, "rebukes the Devourer" (Malachi 3:11). "And I will rebuke the devourer for your sakes, so that he will not destroy the fruit of your ground, nor shall the vine fail to bear fruit for you in the field," says the LORD of hosts. The windows of Heaven open and stay open, praise the Lord!

ONE MORE SECRET TO PROSPERITY

Look at the number three. There are three ways God instructs us to give. When you discover this, your eyes have been opened and you are ready to be a part of God's end-time transfer of wealth—the latter rain.

1. Three First Fruits: Deuteronomy 16:16 states, "Three times a year all your males shall appear before the LORD your God in the place which He chooses: at the Feast of Unleavened Bread, at the Feast of Weeks, and at the Feast of Tabernacles; and they shall not appear before the LORD empty-handed."

2. Three types of giving: Tithes, first fruits, and charity (tzedakah), or acts of kindness. Seek them. Right before God is about to bless you, He first gives you a chance to be a blessing.

3. Three or triple harvest: The final revelation I want to show you brings us back once more to Shemittah.

All giving is an act of faith, whether it is giving First Fruits, tithes, or giving tzedakah to feed children in an orphanage. It takes faith to give. What is faith? It is trusting that God is God—that He will take care of us. It is giving when God tells us to give, saying, "Lord, I put you on the throne of my life." This is why, when Israel came out of Babylon out of seventy years of slavery, God said to them, and to us, "Return—teshuvah—unto Me and I will return to you." "How Lord?" In your giving.

Remember, seventy years of captivity because of seventy missed Shemittahs in 490 years of saying, "We don't need God." They forgot it is God who gives power to gain wealth. Now look at a "truth that will set you free." Leviticus 25:20–21 states, "And if you say, 'What shall we eat in the seventh year, since we shall not sow nor gather in our produce?' Then I will command My blessing on you in the sixth year, and it will bring forth produce enough for three years."

Here again we look at the number three: thirty, sixty, hundredfold. Shemittah, God instructs in Leviticus 25:3–4, "Six years you shall sow your field, and six years you shall prune your vineyard, and gather its fruit; but in the seventh year there shall be a sabbath of solemn rest for the land, a sabbath to the LORD. You shall neither sow your field nor prune your vineyard."

Wow, talk about needing faith. If there is to be no planting and no reaping in the seventh year, then how will we eat that year? Then nothing for the eighth year, so how will we eat that year? The answer is when you trust God, when you know and don't forget it is God who gives power to gain wealth, God says according to Leviticus 25:21, there will be a triple blessing, "Then I will command My blessing on you in the sixth year, and it will bring forth produce enough for three years."

The sixth year is the thirtyfold.
The seventh year is the sixtyfold.
The eighth year is the hundredfold.

Thirty, sixty, hundredfold. Good measure, pressed down, shaken together, and overflowing. God says to us, "Don't forget it is Me who is Lord of the Harvest."

As I am sitting here at my desk writing this, I can't stop without pointing out that verse 21 refers to the sixth year and where we are now on God's calendar. Shemittah, miraculously, begins this year, on Rosh Hashanah, September 24, 2014, which means that right now we are in the sixth year.

Shemittah will last from September 24, 2014, until Yom Kippur on September 22, 2015. The seventh year begins on September 23, 2015, on the last day of Yom Kippur. This is also when we begin the year of Jubilee, on the Day of Atonement.

Leviticus 25:9–10 states:

> Then you shall cause the trumpet of the Jubilee to sound on the tenth day of the seventh month; on the Day of Atonement you shall make the trumpet to sound throughout all your land. And you shall consecrate the fiftieth year, and proclaim liberty throughout all the land to all its inhabitants. It shall be a Jubilee for you; and each of you shall return to his possession, and each of you shall return to his family.

Talk about an appointed time. It's not a coincidence! Remember, the number seven means completion and the number eight is a new beginning. Let your prosperity begin!

7

The Blessing of the Old Paths and Appointed Times

As I've been emphasizing throughout, it's not a coincidence the blood moons fall on the biblical holidays. In the Hebrew language, these holidays are known as moedims—which means appointed times. These are the dates on God's calendar that He has set aside for extraordinary things to happen.

Most of Christianity has never been taught anything about the appointed times, or what Leviticus 23 calls Feasts of the Lord. The revelation has been lost for centuries but now God is sending a sign through the four blood red moons to look up and learn.

The three biggest feasts are Passover (Pesach), Pentecost (Shavuot), and Sukkot, the Feast of Tabernacles. They have been ordained by the Lord for an outpouring of unlimited blessing. These are the First Fruits feasts and considered special Sabbaths. They represent a part of God's plan for incredible increase, abundance, and blessing. It's when the windows of heaven are opened for those who respond.

Ezekiel 20:19–20 states, "I am the Lord your God: Walk in My statutes, keep My judgments, and do them; hallow My Sabbaths, and they will be a sign between Me and you, that you may know that I am the Lord your God."

During these holy days, God commands His people to come before Him, and not to come empty-handed. "Three times a year all your males shall appear before the LORD your God in the place which He chooses: at the Feast of Unleavened Bread, at the Feast of Weeks, and at the Feast of Tabernacles; and they shall not appear before the LORD empty-handed" (Deuteronomy 16:16).

THE OLD PATHS

The significance of this timing is huge! But unless you see it from a Jewish perspective, you'll completely miss all of this! The prophet Jeremiah says in 6:16:

Thus says the Lord: "Stand in the ways and see, And ask for the old paths, where the good way is, And walk in it; Then you will find rest for your souls. But they said, "We will not walk in it."

The Hebrew word for "way"—*derek*—is a very interesting word. Among others, the word *way* means "direction, example, mission, road, roadway, favors, highway, journey and pathway." To better understand this, look at what Jesus said in Matthew 5:17–19:

> Do not think that I came to destroy the Law or the Prophets. I did not come to destroy but to fulfill. For assuredly, I say to you, till heaven and earth pass away, one jot or one tittle will by no means pass from the law till all is fulfilled. Whoever therefore breaks one of the least of these commandments, and teaches men so, shall be called least in the kingdom of heaven; but whoever does and teaches them, he shall be called great in the kingdom of heaven.

Now, look at the word used in English for "law." We immediately think of legalism. We have heard it said over and over again, "We are not under the curse of the law." Galatians 3:13 states, "Christ has redeemed us from the curse of the law," and Romans 6:15 states, "What then? Shall we sin because we are not under law but under grace? Certainly not!"

What is the Lord trying to tell us? Is He saying now that we are saved by grace (and we are), His laws, His Word doesn't have to be followed? No. What about the Ten Commandments—are they no longer in effect? Let me explain what the Bible is and isn't saying. In Greek, the word "law" means legalism. When Paul is talking about "under the law," he is not speaking of God's law, but of manmade law.

I won't go into great detail here, you can read more about it in my other book, *The Torah Blessing.* To put it simply, when the Jewish people came back from Babylonian captivity, and the leaders met in Jerusalem in the Great Assembly, they decided to take God's Word, His teaching, and put a "fence" around it. God said, "Wash your hand before you eat," to be sure we all did it, "man" added detailed instructions to what God said until it became almost impossible for anybody to keep all these manmade instructions.

This is what Jesus was referring to in Matthew 23:4: "For they bind heavy burdens, hard to bear, and lay them on men's shoulders; but they themselves will not move them with one of their fingers."

Again in Matthew 15:1–3: "Then the scribes and Pharisees who were from Jerusalem came to Jesus, saying, "Why do Your disciples transgress the tradition of the elders? For they do not wash their hands when they eat bread." He answered and said to them, "Why do you also transgress the commandment of God because of your tradition?"

I could go on and on teaching on this and it is crucial for you to understand this, but I must move on. So I will encourage you to read my other books on the teaching of the Torah. What Paul is telling us is that Jesus has freed us—not from God's Word, but from manmade laws that lock up the Kingdom of Heaven here on earth.

The word "law" in Hebrew doesn't mean legalism, but rather pathway, teacher, or directive. Look again at the words of Jesus, "I did not come to do away with the law." The word for law that Jesus used in this scripture was Torah—the Bible, the instructions of God to His people. This is what Jeremiah tells us when he says to stand in the ways, stand on God's Word, on His instructions. His Torah, His path, will always lead to safety, to home, to Him.

Before Tiz and I moved our family to Dallas, Texas, we lived in Oregon. Every year we would hear on the news about people being lost in the mountains. Most of the time, getting lost was avoidable. Signs and trails were clearly marked, but for one reason or another, people would ignore the instructions. How many of us have tried to take a "shortcut?" "Yes, I know what the 'map' and the 'GPS' says, but if I go this way…" The shortcut takes twice as long to get there, or worse, we never make it. God wants us to get back on the path. Get back to His "ways" because His "ways" really are above our ways.

HAVE EYES TO "SEE"

The next thing Jeremiah tells us is the same thing that Jesus is telling us, have eyes to "see." Remember the story of Moses, he craned his neck to see [vaya'ar] what God is doing. It is very possible that instead of craning our necks to see what God is doing, we can become "stiff-necked" because of our manmade traditions. Acts 7:51 states, "You stiff-necked and uncircumcised in heart and ears! You always resist the Holy Spirit; as your fathers did, so do you."

One of the things the Devil is most afraid of is the Church, Gentiles' eyes being opened and realizing two things:

First, some of the things we hold onto so dearly didn't actually come from God, but from man and even though we want to walk by grace, we have been put, just like in the past, under the law of man. Jeremiah 16:19–21:

O LORD, my strength and my fortress, my refuge in the day of affliction, the Gentiles shall come to You from the ends of the earth and say, "Surely our fathers have inherited lies, worthlessness and unprofitable things."

Will a man make gods for himself, which are not gods?
"Therefore behold, I will this once cause them to know,
I will cause them to know My hand and My might; and
they shall know that My name is the LORD."

Second, the Devil is afraid that the Church will once again realize that we are Judeo-Christians, as Paul said in Romans 11:17–18;

And if some of the branches were broken off, and you, being a wild olive tree, were grafted in among them, and with them became a partaker of the root and fatness of the olive tree, do not boast against the branches. But if you do boast, remember that you do not support the root, but the root supports you.

We as Christians are grafted into Israel! Galatians 3:29 states "And if you are Christ's, then you are Abraham's seed, and heirs according to the promise [Abraham being the first Jew]."

Now watch this, Jeremiah says, "Ask for the old paths." When God is telling us of "the old paths," these teachings cover every area of our lives from marriage, to health, and everything else we need. But in this part of the book, let's focus on the end-time transfer of wealth—your financial breakthrough.

Whenever a pastor or leader is talking about finances in the Church, he or she will almost always include the book of Malachi. Even if they say, and I have heard this more than once, "That's the Old Testament, we are of the New Testament. The old has nothing to do with us. We're not 'under the law,' now as we receive our tithes."

What we need to know is that Malachi is written, not only for the Jewish people coming out of Babylon, but also for church today. Most of us have only heard part of Malachi 3, usually starting with verse 8, "Will a man rob God?" "In tithes and offerings." This is great, and we need to hear what God is saying, but look at what comes before that in verses 3–4:

> He will sit as a refiner and a purifier of silver; He will purify the sons of Levi, and purge them as gold and silver, that they may offer to the LORD an offering in righteousness. Then the offering of Judah and Jerusalem will be pleasant to the LORD, as in the days of old, as in former years.

Remember this is God speaking to His people after seventy years of Babylonian captivity for not keeping Shemittah, for not remembering it is "God who gives power to gain wealth." The words of Malachi on tithes and offerings are the teachings of the Lord that 10 percent belong to God.

Leviticus 27:30 states, "And all the tithe of the land, whether of the seed of the land or of the fruit of the tree, is the LORD's. It is holy to the LORD." As in the days of old, offerings."

Deuteronomy 16:16 states, "Three times a year all your males shall appear before the LORD your God in the place which He chooses: at the Feast of Unleavened Bread, at the Feast of Weeks, and at the Feast of Tabernacles; and they shall not appear before the LORD empty-handed." This is without a doubt, the missing key to living under "open windows of Heaven."

REST FOR YOUR SOUL

Now look how this all ties together. When we "ask" God for the "old paths," this is exactly what God's people asked in the book of Malachi, at the Great Assembly in Jerusalem. "Look what do we need to do?" God said, "Return [teshuvah] unto me." How, Lord? Return to the old ways: The offerings of old, three times a year, thirty, sixty, hundredfold at Passover, Pentecost (Shavuot), and the Feast of Tabernacles (Sukkot) and prove me if I won't open the windows of heaven—*yesod*— a channel from my throne to you.

Remember the thirty, sixty, hundredfold teaching. God tells us when we "see" and "do," He will first open the windows of Heaven (thirtyfold), pour us out such a blessing there won't be room enough to receive (sixtyfold), and finally He will rebuke the Devourer (hundredfold). Malachi 3:11 states, "And I will rebuke the devourer for your sakes, so that he will not destroy the fruit of your ground, nor shall the vine fail to bear fruit for you in the field," says the LORD of hosts."

When Jeremiah says, "You shall find rest for your souls," the Hebrew word for "rest" is *menuhah*. Look at it as found in Genesis 2:1–3:

> Thus the heavens and the earth, and all the host of them, were finished. And on the seventh day God ended His work which He had done, and He rested on the seventh day from all His work which He had done. Then God blessed the seventh day and sanctified it, because in it He rested from all His work which God had created and made.

After God created everything, the Bible tells us in verse 2 that he "rested" (menuhah). How did God create the world? Did He work and labor to build it? No, He created it, everything, by His spoken word. Genesis 1:3–4 states, "Then God said, 'Let there be light;' and there was light. And God saw the light, that it was good; and God divided the light from the darkness." It's the same with all of creation. God said—and it was. So when we read that "God rested," we need to think with a Jewish mind, not a Gentile one.

Rabbi Abraham Joshua Heschel wrote: "Something was created on the Sabbath and that something was 'rest' or 'menuhah:' tranquility, serenity, peace, and repose. To the biblical mind, menuhah (rest) is the same as happiness, stillness, peace and harmony. It is when wickedness ceases from troubling you and you actually find victory and joy."

So in six days, God created everything: the mountains, the streams, the rivers, the cattle, the birds, and even the world's wealth. Genesis 2:11 states, "The name of the first is Pishon; it is the one which skirts the whole land of Havilah, where there is gold." It was all good. All that our Heavenly Father made was good. He made it for you, to bless you, to take care of you.

But look at verse 2: "And on the seventh day God ended His work which He had done, and He rested on the seventh day from all His work which He had done." Ancient Jewish wisdom says in six days God created everything to be blessed. Jesus said, "Your Father knows you have need of all these things." On the seventh day, He created the blessing.

Here lies the secret we have been missing, as Jeremiah tells us, "Ask for the old paths" as they did coming out of Babylon. "Lord, what must we do?" As you may have been asking,

"Lord, what am I missing for my breakthrough?" Jesus didn't come to do away with God's Word, but to make it come alive, to take if from *logos* to *rhema*. To reconnect us, to redeem us by His blood.

There are seven days that end with the Sabbath (Genesis 2:3). There are seven years that end with Shemittah (Leviticus 25). There were a series of seven four-blood moons that led us to where we are right now—number eight. This is the eighth in the series of four blood moons from the time of Jesus. We have now entered into Shemittah which leads us into Jubilee. This leads us to the greatest time of joy and blessing of the year, the Feast of Tabernacles, but in 2015, it is different. Never again, in our life, in fact, never again in the life of the world, will any of this come again. Look up! Lift up your heads, your redemptions draws near.

My prayer is that if you are reading this book and its ten to twenty years later and the Messiah hasn't come, that God opens your eyes that you too may see. It means we are closer to the coming of the Lord than ever before. The signs in the heavens are truly a warning, a sounding of the alarm from Zion. The four blood moons are a message from your Heavenly Father to you.

8

The Blood Moons
and the Power of Pentecost

And it shall come to pass in the last days, says God, that
I will pour out of My Spirit on all flesh; Your sons and
your daughters shall prophesy, your young men shall see
visions, your old men shall dream dreams. And on My
menservants and on My maidservants I will pour out
My Spirit in those days; And they shall prophesy. I will
show wonders in heaven above and signs in the earth
beneath: Blood and fire and vapor of smoke. The sun
shall be turned into darkness, and the moon into blood,
before the coming of the great and awesome day of the
LORD. And it shall come to pass that whoever calls on
the name of the LORD shall be saved.

—(Acts 2:17–21)

So far, in this book, we have talked about the four blood
moons, prophesies leading up to these "moedims" (appointed

times) and the promise of prosperity—the end-time transfer of wealth. Each one of these topics could be a book in itself. Each is exciting and obviously crucial to God's great love in reaching out to the world with His amazing grace. But what I want to share with you now is going to be the most exciting.

The words that Peter spoke on the day of Pentecost came from the prophecy of Joel. Both foretell of the moon turning to blood. On this day the world began to change. In one moment, three thousand souls were saved, baptized, and added to the church. Now, just the fact that three thousand men received Christ as Savior is powerful on its own, but think with me a minute. What caused this to happen? What got their attention? It was the supernatural—the resurrection power of God. It began with the signs in the heavens.

Just fifty days before this Pentecost, on the exact date of the crucifixion of Jesus, a blood moon occurred—on Friday, April 3, 33 AD. This is absolutely incredible and it's no coincidence it was also Passover. In fact, when I went back and researched this on the NASA website, I discovered there had been a series of six blood moons that occurred on biblical holidays during the two years before and the year of the crucifixion of Christ. You just can't make this stuff up!

BLOOD MOONS THAT OCCURRED DURING THE TIME OF JESUS

Apr 25, 31 AD – Passover

Oct 19, 31 AD – Sukkot, the Feast of Tabernacles

Apr 14, 32 AD – Passover

Oct 07, 32 AD – *Day before* Sukkot, the Feast of
Tabernacles

Apr 03, 33 AD – Passover

Sep 27, 33 AD – Sukkot, the Feast of Tabernacles

They also record a solar eclipse on March 19, 33 AD, just weeks before the crucifixion. This series that we listed above didn't make the list of eight that we've been teaching about in this book because the October 7, 32 AD, blood moon happened the day before Sukkot. Yet this is still a phenomenal validation of God using signs in the heavens. It had to be on Peter's mind when on the day of Pentecost he quoted the prophecy of Joel and the reference to the moon turning to blood.

If all this wasn't improbable enough, the blood moon on Passover 2015 just happens to begin (depending on where you are in the world) on Friday night, April 3, the same date from 33 AD, when Jesus was crucified. Are you convinced God is saying our world is about to change? This is Bible prophecy and God gave it to us so we would have history in advance!

Remember when we taught in Malachi 3 where the Lord said, "Return [teshuvah] unto me and I will return to you." This was spoken to the Jewish about 500 BC. We can't say exactly when Malachi was written, but we do know about the Great Assembly and we can guess that the Temple was either completed or on its way to completion because of God's specific instructions to His people on tithes and offerings: "Three times a year...before the Lord." This special offering would have been brought to the Temple.

Many times we have heard that this was the last time that God spoke to Israel until the time of Jesus because they didn't listen to God, that they didn't "return" and so God was silent for almost five hundred years. I have to disagree. First, look at the tithe. Jesus Himself said they were paying their tithes in Matthew 23:23: "Woe to you, scribes and Pharisees, hypocrites! For you pay tithe of mint and anise and cummin, and have neglected the weightier matters of the law: justice and mercy and faith. These you ought to have done, without leaving the others undone."

Jesus was rebuking some of the leaders for missing the point, but nonetheless they were tithing. Let's look at "offerings besides." Now remember, the Lord is speaking of the offering of old in Deuteronomy 16:16: "Three times a year all your males shall appear before the LORD your God in the place which He chooses: at the Feast of Unleavened Bread, at the Feast of Weeks, and at the Feast of Tabernacles; and they shall not appear before the LORD empty-handed."

The Feast of Unleavened Bread, or Passover, is the time that Jesus came riding into Jerusalem on a donkey. John 12:1: "Then, six days before the Passover, Jesus came to Bethany, where Lazarus was who had been dead, whom He had raised from the dead." Then, "the next day a great multitude that had come to the feast." What Feast? Passover. John 13:1 states, "Now before the Feast of the Passover, when Jesus knew that His hour had come that He should depart from this world to the Father, having loved His own who were in the world, He loved them to the end."

The "Last Supper" wasn't just a random time Jesus got with the disciples to tell them He was going to lay down His life for the world. It was Passover. Mark 14:12 states, "Now on the first day of Unleavened Bread, when they killed the Passover lamb, His disciples said to Him, 'Where do You want us to go and prepare, that You may eat the Passover?'" Israel, and Jesus and His disciples kept the Feast of Passover.

FULFILLING THE PROMISE WITH POWER

Let's look at Pentecost, the second of the three major Feasts. This is also known as the Festival of Weeks, or *Shavuot*. As we all know, Jesus became the Passover Lamb, praise the Lord! Let's take a quick look at what followed. Jesus shows Himself alive. He has risen. I believe this may be the reason Jesus needed to show His disciples the miracle of Lazarus. Why did Jesus delay His coming when Lazarus's sisters called for Him? Could it be He knew that the disciples would be in such a state of distress at seeing Jesus hanging on the cross, at such a state of confusion at hearing Him shout those words, "It is finished!" that they could hold on to the truth?

We saw Jesus raise Lazarus from the dead, but that was not enough. The Bible says that He (Jesus) presented Himself alive. They had seen "many infallible proofs" being with them for forty days, but none of that was enough. Now that Jesus had fulfilled His mission, their (and our) mission was about to begin.

So as we go from Passover to the day of Pentecost, Jesus tells them not just to wait for the promise of God, the power of God, but He tells them to wait in Jerusalem. Why? God could have filled them with the Holy Spirit anywhere at any time. The answer is found in the next chapter, Acts 2:1 and 5, "When the Day of Pentecost had fully come, they were all with one accord in one place...And there were dwelling in Jerusalem Jews, devout men, from every nation under heaven."

Exodus 34:22–23 states, "And you shall observe the Feast of Weeks, of the firstfruits of wheat harvest, and the Feast of Ingathering at the year's end. Three times in the year all your men shall appear before the Lord, the LORD God of Israel."

Deuteronomy 16:9–10 states, "You shall count seven weeks for yourself; begin to count the seven weeks from the time you begin to put the sickle to the grain. Then you shall keep the Feast of Weeks to the LORD your God with the tribute of a freewill offering from your hand, which you shall give as the LORD your God blesses you."

This is why Jesus commanded them to stay in Jerusalem. The Jewish world was gathering there on Pentecost in obedience to God's word in Malachi to return. How? In tithes and offerings. So here we find in God's Word that Israel, in fact, devout Jews from around the world, heard and obeyed God's call to teshuvah, to return to Him in tithes and offerings.

And as we've learned, the last of the three major Feasts of the Lord is Sukkot, the Feast of Tabernacles. This is when we find Jesus in the book of John 7:37–38: "On the last day, that great day of the feast, Jesus stood and cried out, saying, "If anyone thirsts, let him come to Me and drink. He who believes in Me, as the Scripture has said, out of his heart will flow rivers of living water."

Now, what God is showing us not only connects us to what happened at the First Coming of Jesus, but even more for His Second Coming. Remember that everything the Lord shows us has a spiritual and physical meaning and it also has a lesser and greater lesson as well. The Lord Himself tells us this in Haggai 2:9: "'The glory of this latter temple shall be greater than the former,' says the LORD of hosts. 'And in this place I will give peace,' says the LORD of hosts." Again in Deuteronomy 11:14: "Then I will give you the rain for your land in its season, the early rain and the latter rain, that you may gather in your grain, your new wine, and your oil."

Jesus said it this way in John 14:12: "Most assuredly, I say to you, he who believes in Me, the works that I do he will do also; and greater works than these he will do, because I go to My Father." This is why Jesus commanded His disciples not to leave Jerusalem until they received the power. Acts 1:8 states, "But you shall receive power when the Holy Spirit has come upon you; and you shall be witnesses to Me in Jerusalem, and in all Judea and Samaria, and to the end of the earth."

When Jesus raised Lazarus from the dead, the Bible tells us that upon hearing Lazarus was alive, multitudes came to see. John 12:9 states, "Now a great many of the Jews knew that He was there; and they came, not for Jesus' sake only, but that they might also see Lazarus, whom He had raised from the dead." This is human nature. This is God's plan. Prophets with disaster, with signs in the heavens. They may ignore prophecy. Even the wicked may prosper, but nobody will be able to ignore the power of God where He "pours out His Spirit."

Think about John the Baptist. John was called by God to baptize people in preparation of the coming of the Messiah. Mark 1:2 states, "As it is written in the Prophets: 'Behold, I send My messenger before Your face, who will prepare Your way before You.'" By the way, Mark is quoting from Malachi 3. There is a hidden secret here, but that's for my next book, *Breaking the Curse Off Your Money*.

John is baptizing multitudes of people. All of a sudden, his eyes fall on Jesus. John 1:29–32 states, "The next day John saw Jesus coming toward him, and said, 'Behold! The Lamb of God who takes away the sin of the world! This is He of whom I said, "After me comes a Man who is preferred before me, for He was before me." I did not know Him; but that He should be revealed to Israel, therefore I came baptizing with water.'" And John bore witness, saying, "I saw the Spirit descending from heaven like a dove, and He remained upon Him."

Look at the whole picture that we have before us. John was living in the village of Qumran. Suddenly he feels the call of God to leave. He begins to baptize in preparation of the coming of the Messiah: Matthew 3:1–2, 5–6, 13–14, and 16–17 states:

In those days John the Baptist came preaching in the wilderness of Judea, and saying, "Repent, for the kingdom of heaven is at hand!" Then Jerusalem, all Judea, and all the region around the Jordan went out to him and were baptized by him in the Jordan, confessing their sins. Then Jesus came from Galilee to John at the Jordan to be baptized by him. And John tried to prevent Him, saying, "I need to be baptized by You, and are You coming to me?"

When He had been baptized, Jesus came up immediately from the water; and behold, the heavens were opened to Him, and He saw the Spirit of God descending like a dove and alighting upon Him. And suddenly a voice came from heaven, saying, "This is My beloved Son, in whom I am well pleased."

John 1:29 states, "The next day John saw Jesus coming toward him, and said, "Behold! The Lamb of God who takes away the sin of the world!" Then Jesus says to John, "Baptize me, John." John tells Jesus, "It's You who should baptize me." John obeys and baptizes Jesus and "he saw the Spirit of God descending like a dove and alighting on Him and suddenly a voice from Heaven came saying, 'This is My Beloved Son, in Whom I Am well pleased.'"

What an amazing chain of events. The Lamb of God, the Holy Spirit in the form of a dove, God's voice from Heaven confirming, "This is my Beloved Son," but something happens to John. He is arrested and has some doubts. I think the book of Luke says it best in verse 20 of Chapter 7, "When the men had come to Him, they said, 'John the Baptist has sent us to You, saying, "Are You the Coming One, or do we look for another?"'"

I think we can understand John's question. He is about to have his head cut off. He must think I know, I said, "Behold the Lamb of God." I know I saw the Holy Spirit come upon You and I know I heard a voice from Heaven saying you were His Beloved Son, but before they cut off my head I just want to make sure it wasn't the desert heat. Are you the coming one? Are you the Messiah?

The answer Jesus gives in His First Coming is the answer He will give just before His Second Coming. Luke 7:21–23 states:

> And that very hour He cured many of infirmities, afflictions, and evil spirits; and to many blind He gave sight. Jesus answered and said to them, "Go and tell John the things you have seen and heard: that the blind see, the lame walk, the lepers are cleansed, the deaf hear, the dead are raised, the poor have the gospel preached to them. And blessed is he who is not offended because of Me.

I love the answer we see here. Jesus, are you the One? Jesus didn't say, "Well, the Bible says." He didn't say, "Go remind John all that he said and heard at the River Jordan." Instead, He let the power of the Holy Spirit do the talking. That very hour, sickness was defeated, bondages broken, freedom released, and the blind began to see! Then Jesus turned back to John's disciples in verse 22 and says, "Go and tell John the things you have seen and heard: that the blind see, the lame walk, the lepers are cleansed, the deaf hear, the dead are raised, the poor have the gospel preached to them." No one can deny the power of God.

FULFILLING THE GREAT COMMISSION WITHOUT A SPIRIT OF PRIDE

Mark 16:15–20 states:

And He said to them, "Go into all the world and preach the gospel to every creature. He who believes and is baptized will be saved; but he who does not believe will be condemned. And these signs will follow those who believe: In My name they will cast out demons; they will speak with new tongues; they will take up serpents; and if they drink anything deadly, it will by no means hurt them; they will lay hands on the sick, and they will recover." So then, after the Lord had spoken to them,

He was received up into heaven, and sat down at the right hand of God. And they went out and preached everywhere, the Lord working with them and confirming the word through the accompanying signs. Amen.

God confirmed the Word. The Hebrew word for confirm is *quwm* (sounds like "koom"). Sometimes people ask me why I use Hebrew when studying the "New Testament?" Because Jesus didn't teach in Greek, but in Hebrew, or western Aramaic, which is almost identical to ancient Hebrew. Jesus was a Jewish Rabbi, not a Greek philosopher. So when Mark tells us that Jesus would confirm the Word through the accompanying signs, I want to know exactly what confirm means. It means to answer, to come on the scene.

On the day of Pentecost, the disciples, filled with the Holy Spirit, went out everywhere and the Lord rose up and came on the scene on their behalf. This is the reason for the outpouring of God's Holy Spirit. So the "power of His resurrection" will come upon the scene.

I can't close this part of the book without a warning. Just as the part about prosperity came with a warning, so does God's promise of an outpouring of His power. In Deuteronomy, the Lord tells us that we will be blessed to live in a land of great abundance, a land without scarcity.

The promise also comes with a "but." But do not forget it is the Lord who gives us power to gain wealth. Just as the end-time transfer of wealth is part of God's latter rain, so also is signs and wonders. The Lords knows who He can trust with the power that comes with money. He also wants to trust us with the power of the Holy Spirit. Even a greater testing in our life than wealth is power. God doesn't share His glory with anyone. Isaiah 42:8, "I am the LORD, that is My name; and My glory I will not give to another, nor My praise to carved images."

The disciples knew this very well, as we can see from their reaction in the book of Acts and in the City of Lystra (Acts 14). The disciples see a man who had been crippled since birth. He has never in his life walked. As Paul was preaching, he could tell that this man was receiving God's Word and that then the paralytic had faith that he could be healed. Paul, in front of everyone, shouts with a loud voice, "Stand up straight on your feet." With this, the man leaped up and was healed. Now here comes the test! The Bible says that when the people saw "what Paul had done," they all began to shout, "The gods have come down to us in the likeness of man." Wow, talk about an ego boost. The gods have come down. How would you and I handle this? Paul and Barnabas give us the answer.

The Bible says in Acts 14:14–15:

> But when the apostles Barnabas and Paul heard this, they tore their clothes and ran in among the multitude, crying out and saying, "Men, why are you doing these things? We also are men with the same nature as you, and preach to you that you should turn from these useless things to the living God, who made the heaven, the earth, the sea, and all things that are in them.

Paul and Barnabas tore their clothes as part of an ancient Jewish tradition—which today is known as *Kriah*, the Hebrew word for "tearing." They knew pride comes before a fall and didn't want to get prideful or puffed up, so they tore clothes as an act of humility and grief.

Look at another example of this from the book of Acts 16:17–18:

> This girl followed Paul and us, and cried out, saying, "These men are the servants of the Most High God, who proclaim to us the way of salvation." And this she did for many days. But Paul, greatly annoyed, turned and said to the spirit, "I command you in the name of Jesus Christ to come out of her." And he came out that very hour.

I love what it says here about Paul. This girl "greatly annoyed" him and he rebuked the Devil in Jesus' name. I have to laugh just a little. If someone was telling everybody what a great man of God I was, my first reaction may be to say what a "great discernment of Spirit she has." Right! This is why we need to be both strong *and* humble in the Lord. I believe in all my heart that just as the Lord used signs and wonders in His First Coming, "the latter rain will be greater than the former." For this to happen, we need to understand we cannot be puffed up with pride when God uses us.

When the day of Pentecost had fully come, three thousand souls were added, but just over a month before when Jesus was arrested, one disciple denied Him three times, then the cock crowed. Peter and the others were hiding behind locked doors in the upper room. But when the Holy Spirit fell, it filled those who had been in fear with boldness. When they began to speak in tongues—languages from around the world—all who heard it asked what this was. They were all amazed and marveled. Acts 2:7: "Then they were all amazed and marveled, saying to one another, 'Look, are not all these who speak Galileans?'"

Peter stood up with the eleven and raised his voice—the same Peter who said to a little girl, "I don't know Him." But now he was filled with the Holy Ghost and power. The same is true of the eleven, who had been hiding in the upper room in fear. What I want you to see is how the Holy Spirit gives you boldness. One of my favorite teachings comes again in the book of Acts. Peter and John are back at the Temple for prayer in Acts 3. The Bible tells us that they saw a "certain man, lame from his mother's womb." The daily routine was they would lay this man at the gate of the Temple, the Beautiful Gate, and he would ask those coming in and out of prayer for alms. This was a very Jewish practice because Judaism teaches that just before you are about to be blessed that God first sends you a chance to be a blessing.

Peter and John see him in Acts 3:4–10:

> And fixing his eyes on him, with John, Peter said, "Look at us." So he gave them his attention, expecting to receive something from them. Then Peter said, "Silver and gold I do not have, but what I do have I give you: In the name of Jesus Christ of Nazareth, rise up and walk." And he took him by the right hand and lifted him up, and immediately his feet and ankle bones received strength. So he, leaping up, stood and walked and entered the temple with them—walking, leaping, and praising God. And all the people saw him walking and praising God. Then they knew that it was he who sat begging alms at the Beautiful Gate of the temple; and they were filled with wonder and amazement at what had happened to him.

Signs and wonders are not just for the one who needs a miracle, but for all to see. "They were filled with wonder and amazement at what had happened to him." The next thing we see is that Peter and John are arrested in Acts 4:3: "And they laid hands on them, and put them in custody until the next day, for it was already evening." But the word was spreading, as we see in verse 4, "However, many of those who heard the word believed; and the number of the men came to be about five thousand." First we see three thousand saved, and here it is another five thousand.

Now here is the key to the power of the Holy Spirit moving in you, and through you. Acts 4:7–10:

> And when they had set them in the midst, they asked, "By what power or by what name have you done this?" Then Peter, filled with the Holy Spirit, said to them, "Rulers of the people and elders of Israel: If we this day are judged for a good deed done to a helpless man, by what means he has been made well, let it be known to you all, and to all the people of Israel, that by the name of Jesus Christ of Nazareth, whom you crucified, whom God raised from the dead, by Him this man stands here before you whole."

Notice how they gave Jesus all the praise and glory.

Look at verse 13:

> "Now when they saw the boldness of Peter and John, and perceived that they were uneducated and untrained men, they marveled. And they realized that they had been with Jesus." What was the sign to these rulers that Peter and John were men of God? When they saw the *boldness* of both Peter and John, they knew they had been with Jesus. These were the same chosen few who had Jesus arrested and crucified. These guys weren't playing games. Peter, filled with the Holy Ghost, stood up and it was this boldness that proved to them they were true followers of Jesus.

Today, the supernatural power of the Holy Spirit will grab the world's attention and bring them back to the God of Abraham, Isaac, and Jacob. What we read about Peter and John is about to happen again, and the latter rain is going to be even greater than the former. Think about this as you look up to the heavens and see the four blood moons. Seven sets of four blood moons since the time of Jesus and the destruction of the Temple. Seven is God's completion. Now we are at the eighth. Eight is God's number for man living above the limitations of the natural. It's living in the supernatural, it's your time for a new beginning!

9

End-Time Prophecies
for the Church and Israel

I will bless those who bless you, And I will curse him
who curses you; And in you all the families of the
earth shall be blessed.

—Genesis 12:3

Unfortunately, many Christians aren't taught that Israel is
at the center of God's end-time prophetic plans. Many even
believe the Church has replaced Israel in God's plan. Since the
third and fourth centuries, when the Gentile leadership in the
church outnumbered the Jews and we abandoned Jerusalem
in favor of Europe, things were radically changed. New teachings were introduced to separate Jews and Christians and we
need to remember that these were doctrines of men and not
doctrines from God.

Councils formed under leaders like Constantine, like the one in Nicaea in 324 AD, which authorized teachings completely different from anything taught before. At this council, it was decided, through Jesus, all the promises God made to Israel were nullified and given to the Church. In effect, the Church began to teach God was finished with Israel. From that moment, the Jews and the Torah were officially isolated. In fact, Judaism was criminalized.

This is all known as "replacement theology." What this means is that every prophecy in Scripture concerning the blessing and restoration of Israel, especially during these end times, is taught as having been transferred to the Church. It's a destructive philosophy that persists even today.

One of the many errors in this teaching is that if Israel truly has been judged by God, and the Jewish people have been rejected and replaced by the Church, how do you explain the unexplainable—the supernatural survival of the Jewish people over the past two thousand years? How do you explain that despite centuries of persecution, oppression, and exile, the Jewish people have continued to exist and even thrive? How do you account for Israel being reborn as a nation in 1948 after not existing for nearly two thousand years? No one can deny the promises God has made to Israel about being restored as a nation having come to pass, just as the Bible foretold.

The fact is, the Church has not replaced Israel in God's plan. What we need to do as believers is stop, crane our necks intentionally, and see that in these last days, God has not only restored Israel, but He is also restoring the relationship between Christians and Jews. I thank God He called you and me to play an important role in this restoration.

God's plan to restore Israel is recorded throughout the Bible. When Peter spoke on the day of Pentecost, he gave one of the great prophecies on the Messiah in Acts 3:21: "Whom heaven must receive until the times of restoration of all things, which God has spoken by the mouth of all His holy prophets since the world began."

Here God promises to restore everything in the times right before the Messiah's return. This includes the physical restoration of Israel as a nation—in the land God gave Abraham some four thousand years ago. There is also a spiritual restoration occurring right now as well, as the church is beginning to understand and reclaim the Jewish roots of their faith. This restoration is all part of Jubilee, it's part of Rabbi Judah ben Samuel's prophecy and it's connected with the blood moons.

Even some of the world's greatest authors and leaders have recognized Israel's unique role in history. Here are just a few of the many quotes and comments that describe just how important and exceptional Israel and the Jewish people are:

135

Some people like the Jews, and some do not. But no thoughtful man can deny the fact that they are, beyond any question, the most formidable and the most remarkable race which has appeared in the world. (Winston Churchill)

The Jew gave us the Outside and the Inside—our outlook and our inner life. We can hardly get up in the morning or cross the street without being Jewish. We dream Jewish dreams and hope Jewish hopes. Most of our best words, in fact—new, adventure, surprise, unique, individual, person, vocation, time, history, future, freedom, progress, spirit, faith, hope, justice—are the gifts of the Jews. (Thomas Cahill, Irish author)

The Jew is that sacred being who has brought down from heaven the everlasting fire, and has illumined with it the entire world. He is the religious source, spring, and fountain out of which all the rest of the peoples have drawn their beliefs and their religions. (Leo Tolstoy)

A CHANGE OF HEART

This physical and spiritual rebirth is exactly what the prophet Malachi is describing in chapter 4:5–6: "Behold, I will send you Elijah the prophet before the coming of the great and dreadful day of the Lord. And he will turn the hearts of the fathers to the children, and the hearts of the children to their fathers, lest I come and strike the earth with a curse."

As I've mentioned earlier, in Hebrew, everything God teaches has two parts to it—the physical and the spiritual or the heavenly and the earthly. So when it says God will turn the hearts of the fathers to the children, the hearts of the children to the fathers, it's not only talking about our physical fathers, but also our Jewish fathers in the faith.

The children Malachi is talking about represent Christians, who, in these last days, are returning to a love for Israel, the Jewish people, and Judeo-Christianity. We are realizing the truth of what Paul said in Romans 11, that we need to see ourselves as being grafted into Israel. Right now, during this unique time in history, we are seeing something inconceivable—a reawakening around the world of Christians reaching out to Jews, and Jews reaching out to Christians. This has never been seen in our lifetime and really, at no other time in history.

I want you to also notice how Malachi ends. It says, "Lest I come and strike the earth with a curse" (Malachi 4:6). My good friend, Rabbi Daniel Lapin, gave me a great teaching in Hebrew that connects with this so well. He teaches that the sign a nation is cursed is that the children don't know who their father is. In the physical sense, this has to do with illegitimacy. In America today, millions of children don't know who their fathers are. If you have a child out of wedlock, we don't condemn you, but we also realize that this is a curse—a curse that has to broken.

What happens in the physical always follows what happens in the spiritual. The curse of a nation is children don't know who their fathers are. Spiritually, the curse of any nation comes when it forgets who their Father in Heaven is. The curse in the church is that we forgot our spiritual fathers out of Jerusalem and Israel. To break this curse, we need to return our hearts to the Father, and the Father will return His heart unto us.

As soon as Christians begin to walk in this revelation we will begin to experience the full anointing and blessing God wants for us. By rediscovering our Judeo heritage and history, we can and will see a large part of our inheritance restored. This is all leading us into a great and final outpouring of what we call the latter rain. The blood moons are a sign for us to be ready to receive a flood of wisdom, revelation knowledge, wealth, financial favor and signs, wonders and miracles!

This outpouring is what Paul prophesied in Ephesians chapter 2 when he shares his dream and vision for both Jew and Gentile.

For He Himself is our peace, who has made both one, and has broken down the middle wall of separation, having abolished in His flesh the enmity, that is, the law of commandments contained in ordinances, so as to create in Himself one new man from the two, thus making peace. (Ephesians 2:14–15)

God's plan is unfolding right before our eyes. Jews and Gentiles are coming together in a spirit of friendship, unity, and peace, in a way we haven't seen since the first church in Jerusalem. In Hebrew, this is called *aliya*, which in Hebrew means "ascent" and implies the act of going up to Jerusalem. It also has come to mean "return or emigration" which is happening both in the physical, with the Jews returning to Israel, and in the spiritual, with the Church returning to its Jewish roots.

Paul ends his teaching in Ephesians 2 with this phenomenal prophecy:

Having been built on the foundation of the apostles and prophets, Jesus Christ Himself being the chief cornerstone, in whom the whole building, being fitted together, grows into a holy temple in the Lord, in whom you also are being built together for a dwelling place of God in the Spirit. (Ephesians 2:20–22)

What this means is if we're going to build a dwelling place for the power of God to fall, then we have to build it on a biblical foundation that includes both the Old Testament (the prophets) and the New Testament (the apostles) with a revelation of Jesus as the Messiah. The hearts of those in both the Church and the Synagogue need to come back together in peace according to God's plan, and we will see miracles like never before.

WE WILL BE AS THEIR EYES

My twenty plus years of studying the Bible from a Hebrew perspective has been a great adventure of faith. It has broadened and deepened my understanding of the Bible in ways I could have never dreamed of. This journey into studying the Jewish roots began on my first trip to Israel back in the mid-nineties. God spoke to me so clearly on that day in Capernaum.

The Lord told me outside that ancient synagogue (one historians say Jesus would have attended) that He would help me reread the Bible through the eyes of a Jewish Jesus. While I didn't fully understand what He meant or where it would take me, it was an amazing moment in my life. Next to being born again, this has been the most powerful spiritual experience I've ever had. It has changed my life, my family, my ministry, and as we're seeing in these past few years, it's changing the world.

In Jewish literature, it's taught that we are rapidly approaching a major shift in our biblical and spiritual awareness. We are entering into a time the rabbis are calling an Era of Messianic Consciousness, when we will understand everything God says in an entirely new light. This is related to the prophetic teaching on how in the very last days, there will be certain Gentiles whose eyes will be opened. These Gentiles will begin to experience the blessing and favor of God in a way that has never happened before. We will lead the world back to God.

One my favorite places in all of Israel is Jerusalem. When I'm in Israel, I love to walk through the Old City, and I especially love to spend time in the Jewish Quarter and at the Western Wall—the original wall that remains from the Temple dating back to the time of Jesus. It is the holiest site in all of Judaism. For nearly two thousand years, this was inaccessible to Jew and Gentile alike.

In 1967, when the world experienced the seventh in these series of four blood moons, Jerusalem and the Western Wall miraculously changed hands. Today, it is in the hands of Jewish leaders and the Jewish people. You can go right up to this ancient wall, lay your hands on it, and pray. It's a special feeling and a supernatural experience. It's as close as you can ever get to where the Holy of Holies once stood. You definitely feel the presence of the Lord.

Years ago, Tiz and I were fortunate enough to gain access to an underground part of the Western Wall that for many, many years was unavailable. The Israeli government had been conducting an excavation project under the Old City and found a whole new section of the Wall.

Then and now, when you take this tour, you are required to take an Orthodox Jewish guide. In this visit about ten years ago, our tour went through with a female guide. As we progressed deeper underneath the Old City, we each took turns teaching the many historical and biblical facts. But what was so interesting was when I got up and taught about how this all connected to Jesus, this Jewish guide would turn her back on us as if to say, "I'm not going to listen to your religious nonsense."

As the tour progressed and she heard us teach more about the Jewishness of our faith, I know something changed in her heart. As we got to the end of the tour, she spoke about how some day right beyond this spot, the Holy of Holies will be reestablished again and the Messiah will set up His throne. Then as she looked at Tiz and I, she said to the entire group, "And some day if we would all learn to get along and get rid of our differences, God will rebuild His tabernacle."

What a statement of reconciliation! It's a statement we're hearing more and more from our Jewish friends in Texas, in Israel, in Washington, DC, and everywhere. But there is something else in her statement that is so important, something I don't want you to miss. When she said these things, she made a key distinction. In the church we always teach that when the Messiah comes, He will rebuild the Temple, but in reality, that terminology isn't correct.

The correct teaching is exactly what this Orthodox Jewish guide said—tabernacle—God will rebuild His tabernacle. Now why is this important? What difference does it make whether we say tabernacle or Temple? Because the deeper truth here is that she's specifically talking about the Tabernacle of David, and it corresponds to what we're teaching on right now.

In Acts 15, when the Gentiles were first coming into the faith, all the leaders were amazed. They convened what is called the Jerusalem Council. While we can take away many powerful teachings from this chapter, one of the most significant is connected to how they went about describing this amazing turn of events. You see, they were witnessing Gentiles accepting the Lord for the very first time. It was something that had never really happened in their lifetime or their history as a nation.

All the disciples and apostles came into agreement with James, who was the leader, that this was the fulfillment of the prophecy in Amos 9:11, 12. This is recorded in Acts 15:16, 17 and says, "After this I will return And will rebuild the tabernacle of David, which has fallen down; I will rebuild its ruins, And I will set it up; So that the rest of mankind may seek the Lord, Even all the Gentiles who are called by My name, Says the Lord who does all these things."

In the first church the leadership, who were all Orthodox Jews, saw what God was doing among the Gentiles and likened it to the Tabernacle of David. This tabernacle was different from the Temple and unique in three different ways. First, there was ongoing supernatural praise and worship. It was anointed, prophetic worship and it ushered in the presence of God in a real, tangible way.

A second difference between the Temple and the Tabernacle of David was that the tabernacle had no dividing wall between Jew and Gentile. In the Temple there was the Court of the Gentiles and there was the Court of the Jews. There was a wall of separation between the two, but later in the Tabernacle of David, God told David to remove that barrier, because he wanted Jew and Gentile worshipping together.

Finally, it was here in the Tabernacle of David that the Lord heard the supernatural worship and He saw the wall between Jew and Gentile torn down. It was then He came out from behind the veil and began to move with signs, wonders, and miracles. Not just once a week or once a year but every moment of every day. In His supernatural presence, God walked among His people, bringing untold blessing, healing, wholeness, and refreshing.

This ministry and our church family around the world realize we have a prophetic call to rebuild the Tabernacle of David. We are called to teach the Word of God in such a way that it tears down that wall between Jew and Gentile so God can come and dwell with His people. In this supernatural atmosphere, lives will be changed, souls will be saved, curses will be broken, bodies will be healed, and miracles will take place.

Someday there will be a physical building of the Tabernacle of David. But until that day, God is looking for Gentiles who will first build it spiritually, and those Gentiles are going to see the latter rain come upon their lives.

Now watch how this all connects with two of the four blood moons that will occur on the Feast of Tabernacles in 2014 and 2015. The Bible speaks prophetically of the days in which the Messiah will rule and reign, when every nation will celebrate this amazing holiday. "And it shall come to pass that everyone who is left of all the nations which came against Jerusalem shall go up from year to year to worship the King, the Lord of hosts, and to keep the Feast of Tabernacles" (Zechariah 14:16).

This day hasn't happened yet, but this verse foretells of a day when nations will celebrate this biblical holiday. What's so powerful, however, is that even now we're seeing the beginning of this being fulfilled. The Christian nation is returning to Israel and to a love for our Jewish heritage. There's a day coming when the world's attention will exclusively be on Jerusalem. God is allowing you and me to get a head start on what the whole world will do one day. For those who respond, blessings will continue to overflow in our lives.

Let me say that learning our Jewish roots and applying them into our everyday lives is not an all-or-nothing approach. It's okay if you take one step at a time. However, as this great end-time restoration gains more and more momentum, those who choose to ignore or dismiss these things (just as it is with the blood moons) will miss out on the many blessings God is releasing. Some will even experience the other side of this prophetic word in Zechariah:

> And it shall be that whichever of the families of the earth do not come up to Jerusalem to worship the King, the Lord of hosts, on them there will be no rain. If the family of Egypt will not come up and enter in, they shall be no rain; they shall receive the plague with which the Lord strikes the nations who do not come up to keep the Feast of Tabernacles. This shall be the punishment of Egypt and the punishment of all the nations

that do not come up to keep the Feast of Tabernacles.
(Zechariah 14:17–19)

WHO WILL GUIDE US INTO THIS REVELATION?

The prophet Isaiah gave us a powerful word concerning this amazing spiritual change when Jews and Christians come back together.

> Thus says the Lord God: "Behold, I will lift My hand in an oath to the nations, And set up My standard for the peoples; They shall bring your sons in their arms, And your daughters shall be carried on their shoulders." (Isaiah 49:22)

The Amplified Bible says it like this:

> Thus says the Lord God: Behold, I will lift up My hand to the Gentile nations and set up My standard and raise high My signal banner to the peoples; and they will bring your sons in the bosom of their garments, and your daughters will be carried upon their shoulders.

What God is saying, and what He wants you to see, is that this is a prophecy about the Church. It's a prophecy that is already being fulfilled and will continue to be fulfilled until the Lord returns. You and I are playing an important end-time role in making this come true. Because of our love for the Jewish people, courage to stand with Israel, and our commitment to restoring the Jewish roots of the Christian faith, we are helping many in the Jewish community reignite their love for God and for His Torah.

One of the reasons I love studying the Bible from the Hebrew perspective is to receive the revelation God has given rabbis through the centuries. In fact, rabbinically, it is believed there is a 3,500-year continuous chain of biblical knowledge and wisdom dating all the way back to Moses.

In studying the Old Testament, we are able to uncover promises, principles, teachings, and blessings that were always meant for us today and still can have a life-changing effect. This is one of the benefits of learning from Jewish scholars. They bring insight and deeper meaning into specific scriptures that we would otherwise never know.

This is true in the story of Moses and his father-in-law, Jethro, whose name in Hebrew is *Yitro*. As you might recall, Jethro was a Gentile and also a priest of Midian. As we'll see, his place in this story has a powerful connection with the end times and the coming of the Messiah.

To set the stage for this teaching, let me first tell you that in Judaism the first five books of the Bible are called the Torah (and which the church commonly calls the Pentateuch). The Torah is broken down into fifty-four weekly readings, called the *Parashah* or the Torah Portion. Every week, synagogues around the world focus their Bible studies on one of these readings.

The greatest of the Torah Portions is widely agreed to be Exodus 18:20–26, when God gave Israel and the world the Bible. Strangely enough, this Portion is not named after Moses, or even called The Ten Commandments. Incredibly, it is named Jethro-Yitro.

Even though Yitro becomes a family relative, a grafted-in convert to Israel, accepted by Moses as a leader and eventually given a Torah Portion containing the defining event in Judaism, it does seem strange that God chooses to identify this all with Yitro. Yet, when studying this part of Moses' life, you can't help but see God's plan to graft in the Gentiles. Moses, who is considered the greatest of all Jewish prophets, is actually married to a Gentile, Zipporah, who, along with their children, became part of the Jewish nation.

But the question remains, why does the Gentile Yitro end up having so much favor and influence in Jewish history? What is God trying to show us? I believe this is symbolic of

God's plan for both Jew and Christian to share in the inheritance, legacy, and covenant promises of God—all in a spirit of unity, peace, and cooperation.

This explains another secret from Yitro. In Hebrew, his name is derived from the word *yeter*, which means "adding on." This is precisely what God is trying to convey, that the Gentiles will be added on or grafted into this grand covenant of blessing. In fact, ancient Jewish literature records Yitro's amazing testimony:

> What did Yitro hear to make him come to join the Jewish people? He heard about the miracle of the crossing of the Red Sea and the war with Amalek." What was so unique about what Yitro heard? Didn't all the other surrounding nations hear about this also? "The answer is," said Rabbi Yehuda Leib Chasman, "that they heard and remained the same. Yitro, however, didn't merely hear, he took action. Others were moved and inspired for a few moments, but stayed where they were. Yitro picked himself up and changed his life.
> (Talmud, Zevachim 116a)

This ancient teaching points out that Yitro was so inspired that he took a huge step of faith. He joined himself spiritually to Israel. This step of faith in Yitro's life is being duplicated today across the Christian world. People are reconnecting with Israel. It's not about getting caught up into every ritual or tradition as much as it is about restoring the missing revelation to our faith—knowledge that leads to miracles. This can only come as a result of being grafted in.

Now, go with me to the book of Numbers, chapter 10. This is more of the story about Yitro. Again it all ties in with the signs of the end times and the coming of the Messiah. Look at verse 29: "Now Moses said to Hobab the son of Reuel the Midianite, Moses' father-in-law, 'We are setting out for the place of which the Lord said, "I will give it to you." Come with us, and we will treat you well; for the Lord has promised good things to Israel.'"

Here Moses invites his father-in-law, the Gentile, to come with Israel to the Promised Land—which is pretty special. I want you to notice that in this particular text, Yitro is called *Hobab*, which in Hebrew comes for the word meaning love. The change of his name signifies the love Yitro had for Israel and the Torah, something that God is stirring in the hearts of His people today.

In verse 30, Yitro responds to this incredible invitation by saying: "I will not go, but I will depart to my own land and to my relatives." The rabbinical translation of this passage gives us a fuller, more complete picture of what's going on: "Yes I am coming, but I must first go back to gather my people and I will join you in the Promise Land later."

When I'm asked to speak in a synagogue or a Jewish gathering, I'm usually asked something very similar by my Jewish friends. They tell me that I know so much about the Jewish faith and have such a love for the Jewish people that I should convert to Judaism. My answer is similar to Yitro's answer: "Yes I do know much about Judaism and I do have a love for the Jewish people and I'm definitely going to join you in the Promised Land, but it will have to be later because first I have to go and gather my own people—the Church."

Now, in verse 31, Moses replies to Yitro with the most extraordinary request: "So Moses said, 'Please do not leave, inasmuch as you know how we are to camp in the wilderness, and you can be our eyes.'"

Moses is pleading with Yitro not to leave Israel and return home. He doesn't want to take no for an answer. In fact, he is depending on Jethro to help Israel even more than he has already. Remember it was Yitro who taught Moses how to structure and delegate his leadership team to better serve the people in Exodus 18.

What's so phenomenal in his answer is that Moses says, "You can be our eyes." What I'm about to show you is so amazing. In my Bible, it has a little footnote that says the Hebrew word for eyes is literally "guide." In fact, as I looked this up in many of the older translations of the Bible, like the Geneva Bible, it translates the word eyes as "guide." The Wycliffe Bible even translates the word eyes as "leader."

Moses, who as we know is a Jew and leader of the Jews, says to Yitro, the Gentile, "We need you to be our guide or leader into Israel." Moses is saying, "If you'll lead us and show us the way, you will share in the blessing and inheritance of the Promised Land." But hold on just a minute—at this stage in their journey, wasn't Israel still led by a pillar of fire and a cloud of glory? So just how would Yitro, a Gentile, a convert, and a newcomer to the Jewish people, serve as a guide and a leader?

This is where it is so exciting. Ancient wisdom suggests this is actually pointing us to the Messianic Era. It's taught this alludes to the very last days when Gentiles will be as eyes for the Jews. They (we) will be a guide that will lead both Jews and Gentiles together into the Promised Land—into the greatest era of all human history, the era of the Messiah.

It's precisely what Paul is describing in Romans 11:11 where he speaks of God's plan of redemption for Israel and the Church alike. He says God will use the outpouring of salvation upon the Gentiles to provoke or stimulate the Jewish people to jealousy. Verse 12 goes on to say if the whole world has received this incredible blessing as a result of the Jewish people stumbling over the coming of the Messiah, just think how much greater the blessing will be when the Jewish people receive the Messiah.

This eighth series of blood moons are signaling the acceleration of what has already started—the return of the bond between Jews and Christians. Even now believers are returning en masse to the rich heritage of faith begun with Abraham—a love for the Torah and a faith in the Messianic promises of God. For the first time since the early Church, Christians are discovering the proper relationship with the Torah and Judaism.

It's the foundation the prophets, the apostles, and Jesus Himself have built upon. It is all part of our salvation history. This is your opportunity to embrace what God is doing in these last days and connect to the tremendous amount of motivation and inspiration that's being revealed.

10

The Dawn of the Messianic Era

For I do not desire, brethren, that you should be igno-
rant of this mystery, lest you should be wise in your
own opinion, that blindness in part has happened to
Israel until the fullness of the Gentiles has come in.
And so all Israel will be saved.

—Romans 11:25–26

Everything we're talking about here is all leading us into what
in Hebrew is called the Messianic Era. It's the time of the
Messiah; a time when the world will see a great shift in power,
authority and wealth. We have always called it the latter rain.
We call it the end-time transfer of wealth.

Many leading Jewish teachers and authorities have repeat-
edly predicted that when the Messianic Era begins, it will
involve a certain group of Gentiles. These rabbis are saying
that the key to Israel and the world coming back to God

and returning to the Torah (God's Word) is the Gentile—the Christian.

God will open the eyes of certain Gentiles and they will begin to understand and appreciate the Jewishness of the Bible. They will begin to love Israel and the Jewish people, return to celebrating the biblical holidays like Passover, Yom Kippur, and Sukkot, and want to know more and more about these ancient teachings. This is what Jesus is talking about when He says in Matthew 5 that He did not come to do away with the Torah but to fulfill it—to make it come alive!

One powerful Bible prophecy that is connected to this very concept of Gentiles gravitating back to the Torah is found in Zechariah 8:23: "Thus says the Lord of hosts: 'In those days ten men from every language of the nations shall grasp the sleeve of a Jewish man, saying, "Let us go with you, for we have heard that God is with you."'"

Years ago, when God first led me down the path of our Jewish roots, I was given a whole new perspective of the Bible and what has been promised us. I discovered prophecy after prophecy that, in the last days, there will be Gentiles whose eyes will be opened and who will experience a restoration of the ancient biblical teachings. The prophet Jeremiah wrote there will come a day when Gentiles will realize we have inherited useless and meaningless things from our spiritual fathers (Jeremiah 16:19).

In my studies, I came across a teaching by one of the most widely respected rabbis ever to have lived, Rabbi Menachem Mendel Schneerson (1902–1994). He was the leader of the Chabad-Lubavitch Movement. The movement is considered one of the most dynamic forces in Jewish life today, digging deep in the Torah for wisdom, knowledge, and understanding. One of the chief focal points is joy—serving the Lord with gladness. It is said that Rabbi Schneerson guided post–Holocaust Jews from the ashes of that nightmare.

Before he went on to be with the Lord in 1994, Rabbi Schneerson prophesied to a gathering of Jewish leaders that numbered nearly ten thousand. He said as we enter into the Messianic Era God would bring revelation to the Jewish people from the Gentiles, and not just Gentiles, but Gentiles in America. The teaching continues:

> How can a non-Jew have such spiritual power? Many Jews have abandoned the Torah, the word of God, to assimilate or to fit in with the world, to look like the gentiles who did not follow…To look like the gentiles who do not follow the seven laws of Noah or the ten commandments. So as soon as these gentiles come back

to God's word, they will quickly lead the Jews who have strayed, come back to God.

It goes on to say:

The world is now ready for the Messiah. When the gentile is seen keeping God's word, the Jew will ask him, "Why do you do this?" And the Jew will not be able to get that this gentile is keeping the word of God out of his mind.

The gentiles who come back to the seven Noahic laws or the Ten Commandments, they will begin to honor the Sabbath. They will begin to eat proper. They will begin to celebrate Rosh Hashanah, Yom Kippur, Sukkot and Passover. When these gentiles begin to do this, then every Jew will then run to embrace God's word. The gentiles themselves have no idea that they are ready. They have never heard of the seven Noahic laws, but God will raise them up a teacher that will teach them the word of God, and they will bring the Jew back to Israel.

The gentiles don't even know they're ready. They don't even know that God is going to use them, but he'll raise up teachers that will go into the world and return us back so that the covenants can be released." Then, he said, "And Jews will come up to you and say why do you a mezuzah on your door? Why do you pray with a Tallit? Why do you do these things?"

It reminded me of a good friend of mine, a Jewish businessman in the movie industry from Hollywood, California, who called a member of our church and said; "I've been hearing about what's being taught at your church." He said, "Tell me again what your pastor is teaching."

Our member said, "We're teaching people to keep the Sabbath. We're teaching an understanding of Passover. We're teaching folks to understand Rosh Hashanah and Yom Kippur."

The man was blown away and said, "I want you to come to Beverly Hills and meet my rabbi."

So we went to his house and this rabbi had gone to our website and discovered our strong emphasis on Jewish roots.

At the meeting, he asked me point blank, "Why do you have mezuzahs on your door? Why are you wearing a tallit? Why are you eating kosher?" Exactly what Rabbi Schneerson would have said! I went on to explain how we believe in the Jewish roots of Christianity and how Jesus didn't come to separate us from this part of the Word of God but rather to connect us to it like never before.

HOW WILL THEY KNOW WITHOUT A MESSENGER?

Let's go back to Malachi 3, and take a look at something profound that most pastors haven't seen or understood. It's one of the most powerful yet misunderstood prophecies in the Bible. It has a great deal to do with this end-time plan you're reading about. Malachi 3:1 says, "Behold, I send My messenger, and he will prepare the way before Me. And the Lord, whom you seek, will suddenly come to His temple, even the Messenger of the covenant in whom you delight. Behold, He is coming,' says the LORD of hosts."

Most of us have been taught this verse refers to John the Baptist, and more importantly that, Malachi 3 points to the first coming of Jesus Christ. While even I believed this for years, the more I dug into the Word, the more I realized this scripture is more about the Second Coming than it is the First Coming.

Let me explain. Jewish thought and study teach to look for what is called the lesser and the greater. That is to say, many of the teachings in the Bible have both a lesser meaning and a greater meaning, similar to what I've given you on scriptures having both an earthly and a heavenly meaning or application. With this lesser and greater tool of study in mind, the messenger can point to John the Baptist, but I believe the greater meaning of this passage refers to Jesus' Second Coming.

Notice how this text is written, "The Lord, whom you seek, will suddenly come to His temple." When you think about it, there was nothing sudden about the Lord's first coming. Jesus' conception was announced. Mary carried Him for nine months of pregnancy. He was born in Bethlehem and greeted by a heavenly choir of angels, shepherds, and wise men—wise men, by the way, who knew biblical prophecy, observed the stars in the heavens, and made the journey to meet him.

Then Jesus grew up in Nazareth. He was Bar Mitzvah'ed, taught in the temple at twelve, and worked in His dad's carpentry business. The people of His village knew him well and would later ask, "Isn't that Joseph and Mary's boy?" when He went into ministry.

On Passover, He came riding in on a donkey. They watched Him for three days. He was crucified, died, and was then buried. On the third day, God resurrected Him. For forty days, He is seen among them doing many miracles, with signs and wonders. He then ascended into heaven where He is seated on the right hand of the Father. Do you see it? There is nothing sudden about the First Coming of Jesus.

However, Christians know the second coming of Jesus will happen suddenly. In 1 Corinthians 15:52, it is said His return will be in "a twinkling of an eye." According to 1 Thessalonians 5:2, He will come as "a thief in the night." Now that's sudden!

This is why it makes so much more sense that Malachi's prophecy is the about the here and now. It's the greater revelation. It's a call to the church at the end of days to return, or teshuvah. We're the ones who have gone away from God's teachings. We're the ones who need to return to Jerusalem, to our Jewish roots and to loving the Jewish people.

God is raising up leaders—messengers—in these last days who have a knowledge of the prophetic times we're in. Men and women of God like the sons of Issachar who understand the times and the seasons, forerunners who see things before everyone else so they can tell the people what they should do. (1 Chronicles 12:32).

I believe these blood moons are a call for the church to awaken us from any spiritual slumber, to stir us to come to our senses and return to the Father's house. While it's true Christianity has a great deal of returning to do, we are also going to see (and indeed we are already seeing) a shift in Jewish thought as well.

I can only imagine all that God will do during and after the blood moons of 2014–2015. Notice I said *after*. These signs in the heavens were only the beginning of what God had planned. It launched people and even nations into life-changing events that affected their futures for years to come. I believe this eighth in the series is going to do the same. Since history is our teacher and the prophecies of the Bible are true, we are entering into an unbelievable time of power, prophecy, and prosperity. These are the signs that the Messianic Era is dawning. Our future begins now!

ABOUT THE AUTHOR

Larry Huch is the founder and senior pastor of DFW New Beginnings Church in Dallas-Fort Worth, Texas, a multi-ethnic congregation of thousands locally and millions around the world through his television broadcast and live church services online. Larry's previous books include *Free At Last, 10 Curses that Block the Blessing, The Torah Blessing, Unveiling Ancient Secrets Biblical Secrets,* and *Releasing Family Blessings* which was written with his wife and co-pastor, Tiz. Together they have fueled a ministry that spans over thirty-five years. They have pioneered seven churches on two continents.

Pastor Larry is widely acknowledged as a leader on the subject of breaking family curses and restoring the Jewish roots of Christianity. He firmly believes in studying, understanding, and teaching the Bible from a Jewish perspective. Pastors Larry and Tiz are the proud parents of three wonderful adult children (and a son-in-law and daughter-in-law), all who are active in ministry. Their three grandchildren, the "Sugars," are the loves of their lives.

BOOKS BY PASTOR LARRY HUCH

FREE AT LAST 10TH ANNIVERSARY EDITION
You can experience a new beginning today through the revelation in Pastor Larry Huch's classic, tenth anniversary book *Free At Last*. You will learn how to reverse the damaging effects of family curses in your life, your family, your health, your finances, and so much more.

10 CURSES THAT BLOCK THE BLESSING
Blessings or curses, it's up to you. This classic book by Pastor Larry Huch will help you start your breakthrough and remove every blocked blessing in your life. The struggle can finally be over as you revolutionize your life with the truth that will finally set you free!

THE TORAH BLESSING

The miracles you have been waiting for are about to be released through the revelation of *The Torah Blessing*! You can discover the Jewish roots of your Christian faith with acclaimed writer and leading authority, Pastor Larry Huch.

UNVEILING ANCIENT BIBLICAL SECRETS

God's eyes are constantly searching for someone to heal, someone to bless, someone to prosper, and someone to favor. In *Unveiling Ancient Biblical Secrets*, Pastor Larry reveals many of the undiscovered blessings and revelations God has for you, your family, your church, and your destiny.

RELEASING FAMILY BLESSINGS

The family is God's idea. He put it together to keep the most important relationships in life protected and balanced. It is God's intention to bring blessing to families, not just for one generation, but to the third and fourth.

For more information on our ministry products, humanitarian projects, television broadcast, church services online and more, please visit our website at larryhuchministries.com.